IN THE TRENCHES

FINANCIAL SURVIVAL
DURING TIMES OF HARDSHIP

BY CAROL SCHULTZ-WEIL

ILLUSTRATED BY CINDY GONZALEZ

IN THE TRENCHES

FINANCIAL SURVIVAL DURING TIMES OF HARDSHIP

DEDICATED TO

To my family – Mom, Jerry, OJ, Holly, Michael, and Justin, who are all characters in my life story and who now have some of their embarrassing moments in print.

To my friends –Renee and Cassie who supported and encouraged me to write the story and gave me ideas along the way. Cindy Gonzalez who took the time to tell the story with her illustrations. Special thanks to the friend who edited the book and allowed me ask her an endless amount of little questions. Thanks, LeAnn

To those who taught me what I needed to know about living in the trenches and that friends and family are the most important thing- Uncle George and Aunt Isabel, Grandma Tweedy, Paul, Ann, Tammy, Sid and Dick, Cleo, and the town and experiences in Winlock, WA who took a yuppie and taught her how to dig a septic system.

To all those who have been In The Trenches – past, present, and future without whom there would be no reason to tell the story.

And, to Jesus, in whom I live, move, and have my being.

FOREWORD

I hope that I can make you laugh. I hope that I can make you cry. It is amazing how much our finances can impact our lives, our moods, and our relationships. When the changes in our lives bombard us we are often unprepared and one challenge leads to another, and another, and another. It can be like playing dominoes or pick up sticks. It's hard to know which stick to pick up first and you quickly find that choosing the wrong one can impact all the others. You can lose your turn, or worse, you can lose the game and things that you have worked for years to build.

This is not a get rich quick book. This book does not contain all the answers. It is one tool in the toolbox developed from our experiences in the 1980's when the country, for the most part, was going through good times. Currently, we are having our own struggles with the changes in the economy and the nation and find ourselves In The Trenches with all who read this and while many of the circumstances have changed since I began writing this book in 2002, the basic principles remain the same

It is my hope in writing this book that I can offer some ideas that may help even one person get through the game and come out ahead. This could mean saving their home from foreclosure after a job loss. Or, it could mean finally being able to put some money into savings. For someone else it could be just learning to avoid fights with their spouse about money. I hope that all of the struggles that my family has endured and the things that we have learned can help blaze the trail for the others that follow.

This book is divided into two sections. The first has forms and worksheets to help you see where you are, where you want to go, and how to get there. If you are the type of person who feels very comfortable with filling out forms you could even skip to the back of the book where blank forms are printed again. If you are familiar with a computer they can be put on Excel and easily updated and used for what if's. Or, just as easily, you could pull them out, make some copies, and go with the pencil and eraser method.

The second section is a collection of stories and ideas from our family's experience in scrambling to make ends meet when the rope was cut short. I hope that you will take the time to read them because one of the major challenges ahead is creativity and invention for your own unique set of circumstances. By reading the experiences of others it can often give us our own great ideas.

The last page provides my e-mail addresses. I welcome the opportunity to hear from you to let me know what you think works and what doesn't. Maybe we could even kick around some ideas for challenges that have you stumped. I am not a trained economist and cannot make any guarantees but I am a good listener and have been down the road before. You have to deal with finances anyway, so, maybe you can find a way to make it fun and rewarding even during the days of trial.

TABLE OF CONTENTS

SECTION A

GETTING STARTED

The way that a person manages their finances is much more than dollars and cents. It is a picture of the person. Strengths and weaknesses. Habits, hobbies, and priorities are all part of the equation. Personality characteristics like generosity, frugality, will also be exhibited. Are you a planner or spontaneous? It will show up. Do you like to cook or eat out? The numbers don't lie. Do you look for short-term gratification or long-term durability? Have you ever even thought about it?

Working through the worksheets in the next pages is not an effort to change you or mold you into someone else's idea of a good financial manager. Rather, the worksheets are a mirror. What would we do without mirrors? We would have to depend on someone else's idea of how we look. We could only guess that our face was dirty, our hair overgrown, and that we have more lines this year than last. When we look in the mirror we have the opportunity to evaluate every feature and decide if we are happy about it, want to change it, or absolutely can't believe that no one told us about the big patch of dirt on our cheek.

It is surprising just how many things you can do to change your appearance. Your hair can be changed to brown, black, blonde, or purple. It can be short, long, or somewhere in-between. A man can have a mustache, beard or shave everyday. We can wash, put on makeup, pluck, tweeze, or any number of things to affect our appearance. Some minor and some very major.

Finances are the same way. Once we look in the financial mirror we can make almost any change we desire to make sure our resources and talents are accomplishing the things we need, want, and desire.

Going through all the steps will take at least an hour or two if you want a general quick overview. Or it can take hours if you want to get very detailed. Either will work. I spend hours each winter getting it set up for the following year. It is so engrained in my mind that I hardly look at it until the next year when I mark off all the things that I have accomplished. But sometimes when I'm feeling like I'm not making any headway I'll take a quick look at my worksheets and find that I'm not doing so bad after all.

The primary tools we'll be using are:

- The Minimum Basic Budget
- Expense Reduction Plan
- Goals
- Balance Sheet

By spending as little as an hour to look at your financial mirror you may find a way to save your house from foreclosure, find a way to buy the car you have been wanting, or see that you're going the right direction and don't need to change a thing.

THE MINIMUM BASIC BUDGET

As the name implies this budgeting technique helps you to define and clarify what exactly it is you need to live from month to month. It separates all the frills and thrills and focuses on the bare bones of what it takes to keep your bills paid and the hounds away from your door.

Don't think that there is no room for the frills. In fact, after a few months you may even find that you have more for investing, the frills, or all the niceties that you and your family desire.

Most of us spend more than we need to for the basics. The more we can get a handle on these the more we have for the things that we want and desire.

In going through the process you will hear the words needs, wants, and desires often. They are the defining words for our journey to strengthen and maintain our financial situation. They will change through the journey and they will be individualized to your personal and family lifestyle.

I am a number cruncher but I know that many are not so we'll keep it as simple as possible, however, it is one of those things in life we can't seem to get away from. The good news is that the more we become familiar with the big picture the better position we are in to take control of our financial destiny and reach our goals. No longer will you feel that everyone else is controlling your destiny. You will be able to make informed decisions with you at the steering wheel.

Have you ever noticed that at the end of every month you have no money no matter how hard you plan? Month after month and year after year of this gets very frustrating and discouraging. The reason for this is simple. Most people and budgeting plans encourage you to plan every dollar you spend. Unfortunately life is not like this. Every month there is some unplanned expense. A school field trip, a visit to the doctor, extra items at the store, car repairs, or any other of a million things that affect you life. As a consequence there is no money for the expense. You have to scrounge from someplace else or take money from your hard disciplined savings. Finance books I have read say that Americans are at the lowest savings level they have ever been.

Most planners recommend that 3 to 6 months of bill money be kept in the bank. It's a great idea.

But, unless you can get your expenses under your income there is not, and, never will be the opportunity to save. It's called a cash flow problem.

The Minimum Basic Budget form is laid out for one year. Many people end up living paycheck to paycheck simply because they do not have an easy tool to enable them to plan ahead. They assume that because the bills are paid on time this month that they will be next month. Or, if they are late they assume that they just don't make enough money. By completing the form for the whole year it gives a much better picture of the direction that you are headed and also helps plan for seasonal expenses such as property tax, car license tabs, and summer vacations.

The first time you fill out the form complete it as if there will be no changes in your current situation either in added income or reduced expenses. These changes can be looked at later when doing the expense reduction form.

If your mortgage payment is now $750 per month list it in each month. The total for the year would either be the addition of all months or $750 x 12. If you pay electricity only once every two months then list the amount in the months you expect to pay, for example, Jan $350, March $300, May $300, July $200, etc. Total these amounts for the annual total. This allows you to take seasonal adjustments into consideration.

If you are not sure of the exact amounts you spend for something try to estimate and then later you can record your expenditures to see if the numbers are close to being accurate.

Food can be one of the most unknown of all expenses because often there is a trip to the store every day for some item like milk or bread that is never kept track of. Each trip may easily cost $20 as you find additional things you need. Consequently it all adds up but you have no idea how much you have spent. Add to that restaurant meals, ordering a pizza and pop and you can easily blow the bank.

If you don't know how much you are spending on food there are a few easy ways to find out:

Ask for and keep receipts for every purchase and add them all up at the end of the month.

Keep a little tablet where you record all purchases. If you have multiple people in the family making these purchases it may not be the best way to go but if one person does all the buying it is probably the easiest.

Keep an envelope with the money that you plan to spend for food in it. Each time you spend from the envelope throw in the receipt. If you run out of money before the end of the month or pay period either try to do without, or, if you really need the item keep track of how much you spend.

Food is one of the easiest areas to overspend but it is also the easiest area to cut back and get more for your hard earned dollars if you plan and shop accordingly. There is more about this later in the book.

You might notice that mortgage payments are listed in the top section and rent is listed under the expense section. There are a few reasons for this. First, a home is an appreciating asset. It is also a savings account every time you make a payment. As your equity grows your financial picture improves. Rent on the other hand creates no long-term asset. When the month is gone so is the money.

This is not to say that it is never a good idea to rent. In many cases it is the best idea. However, understanding the difference in the short and long-term financial outcome is very important in making the best decision at any given stage of your life.

Once you have the whole form completed the number at the bottom right hand side of the page may surprise you. This number shows you how much money you will have left after paying your basic living expenses for the year. This number is what you can plan to do other things with. Ideally, you want this number as large as possible while still meeting all your basic needs.

If the number is negative you know right away that it is time to take some kind of action. If you don't, you will not only be behind every paycheck but at the end of the year you will either be farther in debt or not be able to meet important needs.

In either case, there is great opportunity once you know what you are dealing with. The following pages will help you see how you can maximize your resources in whatever situation you are in.

Minimum Basic	Jan	Feb	Mar	Apr	May	Jun	Jul	Aug	Sep	Oct	Nov	Dec	Total
Mortgage													0
Property Taxes													0
House Insurance													0
Car Payment													0
Car Insurance													0
Life Insurance													0
Electric													0
Phone													0
Credit Card Min Payment													0
Credit Card Min Payment													0
Sub Total	0	0	0	0	0	0	0	0	0	0	0	0	0
Optional Monthly													
Satellite													0
Internet													0
Debt Reduction													0
Sub Total	0	0	0	0	0	0	0	0	0	0	0	0	0
Expenses													
Apartment Rent													0
Food													0
Childcare													0
Pet Food													0
Sub Total	0	0	0	0	0	0	0	0	0	0	0	0	0
Priorities													0
Total Expenses	0	0	0	0	0	0	0	0	0	0	0	0	0
Income													
Work													0
Other Income													0
Other Income													0
Total	0	0	0	0	0	0	0	0	0	0	0	0	0
Monthly Available	0	0	0	0	0	0	0	0	0	0	0	0	0
Does not include savings, reserve, spending.													

NEEDS, WANTS, DESIRES

Before I married my husband he promised me that he would spend his life trying to fulfill all of my needs, wants, and desires. It was one of the most romantic things I had ever heard because it truly acknowledges the things that motivate us all. He was previously a used car salesman so he did know how to clinch a deal. Shortly after our marriage due to unforeseen circumstances we tumbled into one of the worst financial hardships that I had encountered thus far. We almost lost the house. We didn't have the money for needs, wants, or desires. It took years to get on track and begin to achieve these things.

His words have always stuck with me though and have been the basis for dividing and prioritizing my spending habits. Speaking of prioritizing, it is a great management word that helps you define what is important at any given time and to get those tasks and expenses that are most important done first. We have talked about that in greater detail in the Minimum Basic Budget and for now the important thing to know is that once something is determined to be a priority it then becomes the thing to do first. On the flip side, anything not determined as a priority may have to wait. Sometimes until the next money comes in, sometimes for months, and sometimes it will have to wait so long that the need will be gone completely and it won't get done at all.

Let's define needs:

1. Food
2. Shelter
3. Clothing
4. Health care

That's really about it. We may want to call many other things a need but in reality they are wants. To really make sure we understand a need we must truthfully ask ourselves would I die, or put family or myself in any risk if we didn't have this expense.

Wants:

1. Phone (depending on circumstance)
2. Cars
3. TV
4. Furniture

Desires:

1. Any upgrade on any of the above mentioned items beyond the very basic level. Example, a used economy car will meet your needs but a new BMW will fulfill your desires. Another example, no dessert is needed with dinner

but I really want a bowl of ice cream and the kind with caramel, chocolate, and nuts really would be wonderful.

2. Anything else.

Now using this definition, if you stop and look around your house or look over your current budget and categorize everything you spend or have spent money on in the past you will see that the majority of things that we spend money on falls into the wants or desires category.

I know that you will want to justify why much of your expenditures fall into the needs list. And you could say that you need a car to get to work or a phone for emergencies. Well, maybe and maybe not, we'll get to it later. It is your choice.

I know that just by reading this many are going to squirm and want to put down the book. Don't worry: I'm not going to say that you should sell it all. Just taking the first step to help remind you of the priorities.

The next step while you are looking around at all of the things you have in all three of these categories is to be thankful. So often in our quest for more and better we forget to be thankful. When I was a kid one of the big phrases when we weren't eating all our food was "Remember the children in Biafra." And it is true. Most of us in America, even when we feel poor, are richer than 80% of the world. We may be having a hard time today but good times will probably return shortly. Ponder for a day or so on how much you have in all areas of your life. Let it sink in to the point that self-pity evaporates.

EXPENSE REDUCTION PLAN

Now it's time to get creative; as creative as you can be. Enlist the help of your spouse, friends, children, and books in the process.

Here's the challenge. Come up with at least 3 ways to cut the cost of every single item in your list. Crazy ideas are okay. They may lead to a great idea. Think about it while you are driving to work, taking a walk, or washing dishes. Write down all the ideas and don't even worry about whether they will work or not.

When your list is complete go back through it and try to estimate how much it will save you per month. Now multiply that by 12 to find out how much you could save in a year. A forty-dollar per month savings is $480 per year. Get three or four good ideas and you have a couple thousand dollars that you could do what with?

Putting things in a yearly or annual total also helps to show how the supposedly little things really do add up.

Now all of your ideas have an estimated dollar figure attached and it's time to make phone calls or see if the ideas will really work. Say, for example, that you rent an apartment for $900 and you hope you can find one for $800 per month to save you $1,200 this year. Great idea. So you scour the newspapers and find that the average going rate is now $1,000 per month for rent. So, on this idea it is time to sit back, keep your eyes and ears open, but hold off for now.

On the other hand, after looking at all of your phone bills you find that you have been spending $100 per month on long distance and can't even really remember whom you were talking to. So you decide to cancel your long distance service, buy a pre-paid phone card, and every time you make a long distance call you set the timer on the stove for 10 minutes to remind you to make it brief. (Or you choose this solution because you find that it is actually your 14-year-old son who is really making all the calls.)

In reviewing and implementing your expense reduction ideas it is very important to look for the biggest dollar for the smallest effort. If you have to drive all around town to save a dollar you are not really saving. Once I just changed the brand of feed that I give my horse and saved almost $75 per month with no ill effects or effort.

Interest payments can be one of the biggest expenses that you have without receiving a direct benefit for it. So now is a great time to look at refinance and payoff options on all outstanding debts including your home.

20___ Expense Reduction Opportunities

	Monthly Reduction	Annual Reduction	Income
Total			

20___ Expense Reduction Opportunities

	Monthly Reduction	Annual Reduction	Income
Mortgage - Refinance	100	1,200	
Sell unused vehicles	30	360	2,500
Save on gas by finding local job	40	480	
Reduce long distance phone calls	20	240	
Cut grocery bill by better planning	100	1,200	
Total	290	3,480	2,500

PRIORITIES

These are expenses that come up but are not part of the basic, required, regular expenses. You have some discretionary control over these and no one will beat down your door if you don't pay them. Priorities can be anything from car maintenance to lunch with the girls to gifts to doctor appointments. Haircuts, restaurant meals, espresso, and spring flowers go into this category. Anything that is important to you that is not included in other categories. These expenses can vary in importance depending on many factors including cash availability, how immediate is the need, or how you are feeling at the time. Sometimes lunch with a friend is top priority because one of you really needs the break. Other times, car repairs seem to give us no choice but to put them on the top of the list. Or, maybe that old vacuum has been on the fritz for months and you decide to rush to Wal-Mart when the new sales advertisement comes out.

Determining priorities is very personal and no one can tell you what is most important. They don't always even follow common sense; we just know what we know. Priorities are a place where we make choices, and those choices reflect who we are at any given time and what is important to us.

A sample list:

- Tune up the car
- School photos for the kids
- Friday night dinner and a movie
- New shoes for Joey

There is $100 to spend on priorities so some decisions need to be made. This is what I decide to do:

- New shoes for Joey $25
- Tune up the car $50
- Pizza with husband because we haven't been out for a long time $25

You might disagree with my choices and think school pictures are more important. That's okay. There are often no "right" answers, it's more important to look at your own family circumstance.

The only criteria I use when deciding which of the priorities to do first is to ask myself, "Are any of the things on my list important to the health and safety of my family or animals?" These get done first and I sleep with a clear conscience knowing that I have done all I can do. After that, it is whatever I think is important at the time.

I once postponed getting a new washing machine for three months and took my clothes to the Laundromat instead, not because I never had the money but because there was something I wanted to do more. In my younger years I probably would have panicked that the washer was broken and run out and charged it. And, in the younger years I certainly would have had more motivation to feel that way with children at home.

Another good question to ask yourself when determining which priorities to spend on first is "Will the cost of this item go up, down, or stay the same?" And, "will I be able to make the deal a month from now?" I still kick myself for the time I found the perfect matching area rug for my living room and passed it up thinking that next month would be okay. Yes, I know that it is not critical in the big scheme of things but it was the perfect rug. So the moral to this story is lay away.

It is not the goal of setting priorities to always put the practical stuff first. Sometimes we can choose to delay some practical things and still have an overall higher quality of life in the long run. Family bowling night may be more important than anything else on your list right now.

There are two primary ways to have the money for priorities. Either set aside the same amount every payday or review your Minimum Basic Budget and see which months have surplus. This second method could result in $20 on one payday and $200 the next. It is good to set a limit that you can afford because it forces you to really think about your choices and doesn't let you go overboard.

Anything that is not done on this month's priority list can be held over until the next month. If the same thing keeps getting put on the back burner every month do you really need it? If you really do, such as a car tune up, you will be reminded that you need to get it taken care of.

A notebook is handy to keep your lists in and check them off as they are completed. Then you can look back and see how much you really are accomplishing. Or, you could keep the list on the refrigerator to look at regularly.

It is also a good idea to list any unplanned expenditures on this list. You must have thought it was a priority at the time the money was spent. There were a couple of months that I really got going on Ebay and got really great deals but didn't realize how much I was spending until I listed all the things on the priority page. One of the priorities that month was the Little Golden Books written in French and shipped from Canada. You can see that can't you? I do love Ebay.

Priorities 20___

January	Cost	X

February	Cost	X

March	Cost	X

April	Cost	X
Shrubs	30	
Oil Change	30	x
Lunch w Tracy	10	x

May	Cost	X
shrubs	30	x
vet	50	x
kitchen curtains	20	x
paint for kitchen	50	x

June	Cost	X

July	Cost	X
Birthday Present	20	x
Doctor Bill	100	x

August	Cost	X

September	Cost	X

October	Cost	X
rugs	30	x
Chinese Dinner	50	x

November	Cost	X
Christmas	200	x

December	Cost	X
Christmas	300	

GOALS

We talk about them, we think about them, but when it comes time to write them down we draw a blank and say that we have none. Why is this? Often it is because even in our thinking we attach a "but" to the end of the goal. "I would like to get a new outfit, but, I don't have any money". Or, "I would like to have a nice yard, but, I don't have the time". We have defeated and excused ourselves all in one sentence. It also gives us a defense of why we are never moving forward.

Writing goals down and reviewing them regularly is often the first step in making them happen. Almost like magic they start to get done. It is not really magic, it is reminding us, keeping the goal in mind, and then our actions begin to line up with our desires. From this first step we can also give ourselves a nudge by making plans, setting aside the time and money to accomplish them.

The next exercise is to write down some of the goals we wish to accomplish in the next year. Do yourself a favor and write some down that you know are easy and free. As you cross these off your list and feel the sense of accomplishment it makes the other harder ones seem more possible. The only thing that holds us back are the limits and excuses we allow ourselves to have. Some goals may be accomplished in a day and others may take months or even years to complete. If we keep them before us we will get them done. If months and months pass and no effort is made then maybe we really didn't want to do it in the first place. Maybe we just thought it sounded good to ourselves or others, or, it was something we thought we "should do". Often we let others tell us what we should do and although we really don't want to we continue to give the subject lip service.

An example of some of my goals in past years:

1. Plant a vegetable garden.
2. Go to church every week.
3. Have friends over for dinner once a month.
4. Get a newer car.
5. Clean out the garage.
6. Paint the living room.
7. Buy one $25 savings bond each month.

You will notice that many of these cost little or no money. Even though this book is about finances the most important thing is to maintain a balanced happy life. Goals that don't cost money remind us that life itself is good and that keeps us in perspective.

My next step is to attach a cost to the ones that do have expenses.

1.	Plant a vegetable garden.	$25
2.	Go to church every week.	Free
3.	Have friends over for dinner once a month.	Free
4.	Get a newer car.	$9,000
5.	Clean out the garage. Cost of dump.	$100
6.	Paint the living room.	$100
7.	Buy one $25 savings bond a month	$25 per month

I love the word free. Most of us do. It brings such a sense of relief and other good feelings.

As I review the list I see that most of my goals are fairly easy to accomplish. The hardest one will be to purchase a newer car because I know that I have no money in savings. So, I know that I must start doing some research. How much is my old car worth? When is the best time to sell it? Should I trade it in? What kind of car should I get?

After researching I decide that I should sell my old car, buy a good used car from the paper, and obtain financing from the bank on the difference. I know that I don't have too many debts because I have done all the Minimum Basic Budget and expense reduction ideas. I am in pretty good shape to take on this monthly payment. I decide to take my cousin shopping with me because he knows much more about cars than I do. Within a few months I have sold my car, bought a newer one in great shape and the monthly payments are low enough that I can afford to pay extra each month.

I finished goal #5 and can now put my new car in the garage that was once filled with junk.

My lettuce did great and I gave away plenty to neighbors but the tomatoes froze before they were ready.

I have had lots of fun with having friends over. I did miss some church but got there most of the time. And, I now have $225 in savings bonds that will be worth $450 down the road.

Goals are great. They help us to accomplish the things that we have really wanted to do.

Goals 20___

		Estimated Cost
1		
2		
3		
4		
5		
6		
7		
8		
9		
10		
11		
12		
13		
14		
15		
16		
17		
18		
19		
20		

THE BALANCE SHEET

Ho Hum. I know that it just sounds boring already. But it only takes about 10 minutes. It doesn't have to be totally accurate; estimates will do. The balance sheet gives a valuable, often eye opening, tool so that you can see where you are and where you want to go.

Face it. Most of us resent bankers, even just a little. Why? Because they take our money, use it, make a big profit, and hassle us if we want to borrow from them. Bankers are often criticized for their strictness, rules, and all the hoops that people have to go through to borrow money. Why do they do this? They insist on making money. They are often more concerned that they make money off our money than we are. So that is exactly what happens. They make money off our money and year after year we feel like we are running in place. Lots of effort, but going no place. If we began to be as concerned that we make a profit as the banks are then there might be some big changes.

The balance sheet can help you easily see what you need to see to change all that. So, please take a few moments to fill in the blanks. Extra lines are provided for things not listed.

Don't forget the personal loan from your parents and the savings bonds you have had stashed away since you were a child.

The balance sheet is to finances like a scale is to dieters. This is just a starting point. Whether you like the numbers or not it shows where you are and what all of your hard work is getting you.

20__ Balance Sheet

Assets   **Liabilities**

Assets		Liabilities	
House		Mortgage	
Vehicle #1 Value		Vehicle #1 Amt owed	
Vehicle #2 Value		Vehicle #2 Amt owed	
Vehicle #3 Value		Vehicle #3 Amt owed	
Jewelry		Credit Card #1	
Furniture		Credit Card #2	
Savings		Credit Card #3	
Stocks		Personal Loan	

Total _____   _____

Net Worth   (assets minus liabilities)   _____

CRITICAL CHOICES

Why is it that some people always seem to be doing well and have money and others are always short and just trying to make ends meet? The most common way that people would answer this question is MORE INCOME. The average person is always trying to get more. Striking workers always say how they just can't make it on their income. It is often heard that the COST OF LIVING is going up too fast. While these things are often true, of greater importance and impact is not how much we make but rather how we choose to SPEND.

The following pages are samples of balance sheets for two young couples. In our example we will assume that both make the same amount of money, have the same number of children, and live in the same area. Both are doing the best they can and trying to spend their money wisely. There are three important differences in the way they spend. The outcome of these choices will quickly be seen.........

Couple 1

Housing	Finds a house in the area that has been run down, vandalized, and in need of repair. The asking price is $100,000. They have a savings and make an offer of $80,000 with 20% down. The offer is accepted and their monthly payment is $425.
Cars	They scour the papers for a good used vehicle and pay cash. They prefer an older car because it keeps the cost of insurance down and since a car is a depreciating asset they do not want to tie up more of their money than they have to.
Furniture	Garage sales every Friday to find the perfect piece for each nook and cranny of their new home. They add these pieces to the ones they received from family when they first started out.
Cashflow	In these 3 items couple 1 now has $790 more per month to spend than couple #2. They choose to use this money to fix up their home, put $100 in savings, and 2% of the husband's earnings go into the company profit sharing plan with his employer matching all contributions. They are able to enjoy a two week vacation every year and buy a beautiful new ring for his wife on their 5th anniversary.

Couple 2

Housing	Finds a house in the area that is identical to couple #1 except that it is in excellent condition, has a fresh coat of paint, and the yard even has a nice swing set that their daughter loves. They are able to make a 10% down payment by borrowing from their dad and agree to the asking price of $120,000. Their monthly payment is $718.
Cars	They purchase a new economy car at $15,000 on a five year term. They use their old car for a trade in and their monthly payment is $297 per month plus $75 more in insurance than couple 1 pays.
Furniture	Watches for a sale at the local furniture store. They are able to furnish the whole house with $5000 that they put on their account. They love to walk through their new home and entertain lots of guests to show off.
Cashflow	Couple number 2 finds themselves constantly falling short on cash no matter how hard they try. In the next 5 years they end up charging $10,000 for unexpected and unplanned expenses such as replacing the washing machine, car repairs, holiday gifts, new school clothes for the kids. Every month things just seem to be getting harder and they just don't understand why or what to do to improve the situation. Lately they have both been looking for other jobs so they can earn more money.

Couple 1

200_ Balance Sheet

	Assets	Liabilities	Notes
House	$80,000	$64,000	20% down fixer. Payments $425 per month
Car	$5,000	$0	Cash
Furniture	$1,000	$0	Garage Sales, family giveaways, cash.
Jewelry		$0	
Stocks		$0	
Savings		$0	
Total	$86,000	$64,000	
Net Worth		$22,000	

Couple 1

200_ Balance Sheet
5 years later

	Assets	Liabilities		Notes
House	$145,000	$60,200		
Car	$2,000	$0		
Furniture	$1,000	$0		
Jewelry	$1,500	$0		
Stocks	$5,500	$0		2% of husband's salary plus employer match
Savings	$6,000	$0		$100 per month
Total	$161,000	$60,200		
Net Worth		$100,800		
				This couple has $790 per month more to spend than couple 2 even though they both make the same.

Couple 2

200_ Balance Sheet

	Assets	Liabilities	Notes
House	$120,000	$108,000	10% down. $718 monthly payment
Car	$15,000	$14,000	Trade in old car. Loan on balance. $297 pymt.
Furniture	$5,000	$5,000	Credit Card 0% down
Jewelry	$5,000	$5,000	Credit Card 0% down
Stocks	$0	$0	
Savings	$0	$0	
Total	$145,000	$132,000	
Net Worth		$13,000	

Couple 2

200_ Balance Sheet
5 years later

	Assets	Liabilities		Notes
House	$145,000	$101,500		No improvements. Appreciate at market rate.
Car	$5,000	$0		Depreciates at same rate of payments
Furniture	$1,500	$0		5 year old furniture worth 25% of original price
Jewelry	$5,000	$5,000		Credit card minimum payments made.
Credit Card Debt	$0	$10,000		Charge $2000 year. Minimum payments made.
Stocks	$0	$0		
Savings	$0	$0		$100 per month
Total	$156,500	$116,500		
Net Worth		$40,000		

WHEN THE BALANCE SHEET SHOWS A NEGATIVE NUMBER

If this is the first time you have ever done a balance sheet the results will probably surprise you. If all your economizing results in a large positive number you will be patting yourself on the back.

But, what if you find that you have a negative number? Just what does that mean? Quite simply, whatever you have been spending your money on is now gone. It could be food, entertainment, or other short-term necessities. Or, it could be doctor bills in which the benefit cannot be measured in dollars and cents even though the bills can.

The first step is to figure out where your money is going. If you have done the Minimum Basic Budget you should have a pretty good idea but here are some of the possibilities:

1. Rent.
2. Entertainment.
3. Alcohol, drugs, or cigarettes.
4. Gambling.
5. Credit Card Interest.
6. Gifts or Contributions.

7.   Fast food or other restaurants.

8.   Your ex-spouse.

9.   A hobby.

10.   Clothes.

11.   A spouse that spends on any of the above.

Once you know the primary areas that your money is going you can then decide if that is where you want it to continue to go. Each person has the right to choose their lifestyle and habits. But, recognize that by choosing one way to spend you are giving up other things. Many people complain that they don't have enough money but fail to acknowledge that the reason they do not have much is because they spend it on some of the above-mentioned items. You might not want to acknowledge it but everyone around you knows because these things are clearly noticeable. You might as well admit them.

Other things that may have affected your finances are:

1.   Divorce.

2.   Illness.

3.   Job lay off.

4.   Slow economy.

5.   Family needs.

6.   Medical bills.

7.   Tragedies such as fire, flood, drought.

8.   Lack of knowledge about money matters.

Until you can determine the primary factors that have affected your finances you will not be able to decide what steps you can or want to take to change them. You can nickel and dime yourself to death with budgets, counting costs, and worry, or try to change the little things but if you are able to identify and change the big things then the little things will come much easier.

So,

Step 1. Identify the major things that have impacted your finances.

Step 2. Decide if you can or want to **change** these things.

Step 3. Make an action plan or goal to **change** them.

Step 4. Get the help you need to put your plan into action.

Sep 5. Put the plan into **action**.

Financial planning is not and cannot be a one size fits all approach. Our lives, needs, wants, desires, skills, talents, and personalities are all too different. What works for me may put you farther behind or cause you to neglect vital needs in your life. So, while you do want to get advice, read books, talk to friends about finances, remember that you have to make your own plan.

Back to things that impact finances. A few examples:

Joe looks at his finances and realizes that he spends $100 every weekend on beer, pizza, dates, going to the car races. That's $400 per month. Joe is young, single, works hard during the week and that's just what he wants to do and doesn't want to change. In fact, he would like more money to do more of this with. Okay, for Joe then we will categorize this spending as Priority because that is Joe's priority at this time of his life. That is not an area he wants to change right now.

John on the other hand looks at the same $100 per week and feels like he has been slapped in the face because he didn't realize that his drinking has had such an impact on his life. John decides to set himself a limit of $20 per week and if he has any trouble meeting that goal he plans to go to a support group to help him out.

Mary is surprised that after all her hard work she has so little to show for it and decides to get more information about how to manage money by reading books and attending seminars as they come up. She is already 40 and better get busy now if she wants to be ready to retire.

Carol loves to read and is surprised to find that she has spent $225 on books so far this year. She decides to start going to the library and second hand bookstores.

Mike just got a divorce and lost everything including his credit rating. Not only that, but, now he has to pay 33% of his income for child support for the next 15 years. Mike feels like he is starting over because he is. And, starting over in the hole. He is overwhelmed and decides to just throw the bills in the corner, have a beer and forget about it. Did you get that word? DECIDES. It is a very important word, an **action** word. Should we all feel sorry when a year from now they repossess Mike's truck? Until Mike DECIDES that he wants to deal with his finances in a positive way he will continue to fall behind. Pity the poor woman who comes along and thinks that Mike is cute. The good news for Mike is that he can make a new decision each and every day that he wakes up so no matter how much he messes up today, tomorrow he can change his mind.

There are as many examples as there are people. When I wrote the steps notice the words in bold? **CHANGE** and **ACTION**. We can whine as much as we want. Sometimes it really does make us feel better. But until we decide to **change** and take **action** nothing is going to get better, it may even get worse.

There are countless good resources available to teach, help, and support us in achieving our goals.

NOT EVERYTHING
THAT GLITTERS IS GOLD

So you have been looking for a job for months and the bills are way behind. Creditors are calling and the mortgage payment is late. Finally you get two offers.

The first is at a small office 10 miles from home. They offer to pay you $8.50 per hour and in a year there might be an opportunity for advancement. They have a one-hour lunch break and the people in the office seem really nice. They are a professional office so nice clothing should be worn daily. Jeans on Fridays are okay. It is more entry level than you have had in the past but it's a job.

The second offer was from McDonalds. One day last week as a last resort you put in an application when you walked over with your kids for a treat that you couldn't really afford. You say to yourself "Thank God I don't have to take that job." But for discussion sake let's look at it. They pay $6.95 per hour with a 25 cent raise in 90 days. They would supply those ugly uniforms for you that you don't really want to be caught dead wearing. They said that they would give you any schedule you wanted because they had a few openings and they would be happy to have someone with your skills.

Just for a minute let's look at the numbers. The samples on the following pages show all the income and all the expenses for taking each job. The only items I have left out are taxes and any voluntary deductions you might sign up for.

For those of you who don't like to look at charts, here are the highlights:

1. You can have $800 dollars more per year by taking the McDonalds job.

2. AND, you only have to work 30 hours instead of 40 to do it.

3. This means, that you will have 912 more hours this year to do what you want.

4. If you primarily use your car to get to work and can possibly get by without one for a year you can have the value of the car and the monthly savings on maintenance and insurance to help you get your mortgage payments caught back up.

5. You don't need to find childcare because you can be home when your kids get home.

A couple of principles are at work here that we often forget about:

1. We have to look at the whole picture, not just the stated salary.

2. The facts must be customized to your own family. No two families are exactly alike.

3. Long term goals and short-term needs must be in balance. It's great to have "career potential" but don't lose your house for what might happen someday. If the bills are due now then figure out the best way to pay them. Or another way to say it. A bird in the hand is worth two in the bush.

4. Remember that it is the companies with the "career potential" which are now doing all of the lay-offs.

Before we close this subject: you may have made an excellent salary in your last position. It may be terribly hard to consider going to a minimum wage job knowing where you came from and what your skills are. No one is suggesting a career change. Just a way to get by until things turn around.

My mom was an RN her entire career and I believe she was one of the best. Her specialty was care of cancer patients. Years after I was an adult she told me that during the nursing strike of the 1970's she had to find another source of income.

She worked as a motel maid for a time to make ends meet. ALL HARD WORK HAS HONOR. I have always been proud of my mother for being a nurse but just as proud that she was a housekeeper when her family needed it.

If you have worked on the Minimum Basic Budget you can take any legal money making opportunity and decide if it will meet your basic needs. Better to have a smaller amount of money coming in the house than no money at all. I will provide a blank work sheet so that you can do your own comparisons. The fast food restaurant down the street may be a much better job than you give them credit for.

JOB PROFITABILITY WORKSHEET

		Weekly	Monthly	1 year
Income/ Credits	Gross pay			
	Tips			
	Employee benefits			
	Employee discounts			
	One time Income/credits (put in 1 year column)			
	Total Income			
Expenses	Taxes			
	Gas			
	Clothes			
	Personal care products			
	Childcare			
	Lunches			
	Office expenses (gifts, parties)			
	Your special treats (coffee, morning donut) Other:			
	Total expenses associated with this job			
Net Income	Subtract expense total from income total			
Hours Spent	Work			
	Lunches			
	Commuting			
	Buying gas			
	Other:			
	Total hours			
Actual rate per hour	**Divide Net income by total hours**			

*the average monthly days worked is 21
Monthly hours worked is 173

JOB PROFITABILITY WORKSHEET
McDonalds

		Weekly	Monthly	1 year
Income/ Credits	Gross pay @ 30 hours week 9am to 3pm	$208	$876	$10,790
	Tips			
	Employee benefits daily lunch credit	$17	$70	$844
	Sell car			$2,000
	Eliminate cost of license			$30
	Eliminate car maintenance			$250
	Reduce car insurance			$480
	Total Income			$14,394
Expenses	Gas			
	Clothes			
	Childcare			
	Lunch out every Friday with co-workers			
	Your special treats (coffee, morning donut)			
	Other:			
	Total expenses associated with this job			$0
Net Income	Subtract expense total from income total			$14,394
Hours Spent	Work	30	126	1,512
	Lunches	0.5	2.5	126
	Walk to work	10 min	3.5	42
	Buying gas			
	Other:			
	Total hours			1680
Actual rate per hour	**Divide Net income by total hours**			$8.57
	*the average monthly days worked is 21 Monthly hours worked is 173			

JOB PROFITABILITY WORKSHEET
Office Job

		Weekly	Monthly	1 year
Income/ Credits	Gross pay	$340	$1,470	$17,680
	Tips			
	Employee benefits			
	Employee discounts			
	One time Income/credits (put in 1 year column)			
	Total Income			$17,680
Expenses	Gas	$10	$40	$480
	Clothes		$25	$300
	Personal care products			
	Childcare	$100	$400	$4,800
	Lunch out every Friday with co-workers	$10	$40	$480
	Sack lunch 3 days a week	$10	$40	$480
	Your special treats (coffee, morning donut)		$10	$120
	Other:			
	Total expenses associated with this job			$6,660
Net Income	Subtract expense total from income total			$11,020
Hours Spent	Work	40	173	2,076
	Lunches	5	21	252
	Commuting	5	21	252
	Buying gas		1	12
	Other:			
	Total hours			2592
Actual rate per hour	**Divide Net income by total hours**			$4.25

*the average monthly days worked is 21 Monthly hours worked is 173

SECTION B

MILLIONAIRES AMONG US

I have known three millionaires who were friends or family. These are my observations. Maybe you know some also and you can see if you agree or can draw your own conclusions.

1. Two of the three started with an inheritance. I don't mean that their parents necessarily were dead. One built his first small house, with cash, on his parents land so had no housing expense until he built his own larger house with saved cash. The second became part of the family business. The parents of these two individuals did not wait until they died to help their grown children get a good start. In many ways this tradition has been replaced by parents paying for a college education that they hope will provide a greater earning potential. The third man was an immigrant who came to this country with nothing and first opened his own butcher shop and then landscaping business. This business eventually catered to the wealthy housing areas and commercial properties. It was funny that this little old Asian man in the dirty clothes and old truck had just as much money in the bank if not more than the people he served.

2. Two of the three owned their own business and then later businesses and land. These businesses where considered blue collar until their attention turned to investors. The one who worked for someone else had a stable truck-driving job that he held for 40 years.

3. Debt. All stayed out of debt and didn't pay interest on purchases. Including businesses or houses. The story was often told of my uncle who totaled his car while on a trip. He went to the closest car dealer and drove home a brand new car that he paid for in cash.

4. Cars. All had nice newer cars that they maintained well. All also had a second car that was a utility vehicle that was dirty all the time and either very economical or functional depending on the primary use. Their nice cars were the "weekend" car.

5. Clothes. None spent much on clothes. They wore their clothes out or continued to wear them after they were already mended and worn out. When they did finally break down and buy new work clothes they bought a dozen of the same kind of shirt to last the next 10 – 15 years. They did have a few nice clothes for social events and business meetings.

6. Houses. All bought their houses in cash after saving up to do so. They were conservative homes that they lived in most of their lives. They were not concerned about trad-

ing up though they did have the amenities they wanted. They maintained their homes well and didn't worry about resale value because they did not plan to move.

7. Furniture. All bought quality furniture that they kept for their lifetimes.

8. Food. All ate very well but did not spend much in restaurants. They ate to live not live to eat. Their food was basic and they always had lots stored in the house. Usually 6 months to a year supply.

9. Buying. All negotiated prices on what they purchased and got it cheaper than the asking price.

10. Stuff. None spent much on "stuff" or grown up toys. If and when they did take a vacation they could travel anywhere in the world but they did not have boats, snowmobiles, RV's or other non essential things.

11. Social. All had active social lives. This included barbeques in the backyard and bridge club. Once a year or so they would splurge and go out dancing.

Each of these men grew financially successful as the years passed. They were extremely hard workers who lived conservatively and were very practical. They enjoyed the simple things in life such as family and good food and didn't get caught up in all the latest fads and popular activities.

There is nothing that any of these men did that the average person could not do if they choose to. So it wasn't luck, the big break, or any other random act that caused them to be financially successful.

So here we have a landscaper, a truck-driver, and a sawmill worker who became millionaires. Is it really impossible or just a lucky break?

THE WORST POSSIBLE TIME

Almost all of us will go through a financial hardship at some time in our lives. Many times it is unexpected and sometimes we have seen it coming but shoved it out of our minds believing we were doing ourselves a favor by not worrying. So when the hard times come we are not prepared.

The worst part of financial problems is that they are often coupled with some other family tragedy. The abandonment of a spouse, the injury, disability, or death of a family member, or the loss of a job, maybe one that has been held for 20 years.

When we are least able to emotionally handle financial problems and our creativity is overcome by shock or sorrow the clock begins ticking on our financial decline. Even if we have reserves we tend to think that the troubles will be over soon but our hard saved reserves dwindle away at a pace much faster than we were able to put them away.

Unfortunately the time to act is now. Your life may feel like the bottom has fallen out or is on hold but each day that has passed without action makes it harder to get a hold of the finances and harder to catch up if you get behind. They can be like a snowball going downhill gaining momentum as it goes.

Because you have probably just experienced one major change thinking about or changing your finances is probably the last thing you want to think about. In fact, you might even resist any more change just to try and feel like there is something in your life that you still have control of.

Recent situations may have caused you to deal with finances for the first time in your life. And it is truly overwhelming. The sink or swim method of financial instruction.

Some people have a short time of hardship and are able to get things under control in a couple of months. But I have found that when I have been without income for even one or two months it may take almost a year to get back to the level I was at before the problem. For others the financial hardship can go on year after year. Barely making it and never getting ahead.

I remember attending many seminars that were supposed to be about financial management and the first topic was investment. Yeah, right. I just wanted to get the bills paid on time. With all the books, seminars, and discussions very few even touched on the challenges I faced.

Whatever the cause, whatever the reason, you probably really don't even want to deal with it. In fact it is probably the last thing you want to deal with. It is a time when all the motivational tapes just don't cut it. Unfortunately these are the exact times when we have to face it. Deal with it or lose it all. And all the while there is a struggle that may include fear, anger, frustration, disappointment and denial.

So whether this information helps you deal with the next 90 days or the next 10 years I just hope it helps. There are no guarantees, no motivational upbeat promises, just a time to take action.

ONLY IN AMERICA

As I have worked on this book I have often thought how utterly preposterous these ideas would be in any country but America. If we lived in many countries around the world our only goal for the day would be to keep ourselves and our families from starving.

This is a very important point so I hope you will give it much thought. It is so easy to limit our own options and blame someone or something else for our situation. We can create our own prison of self-pity and hopelessness within our minds. I love the prayer made popular by AA and often pray it: "God grant me the serenity to accept the things I cannot change, the courage to change the things I can, and the wisdom to know the difference".

Only in America can we go to the library and look at the internet for free and find a job or a home across the country. We can then purchase an airline ticket for under $100 to almost anywhere in the country. Do you realize what freedom this is?

We can begin a whole new life for ourselves for under $100.

Yes, it can be risky and it can be hard, but it is possible. We cannot expect someone else to work it all out for us and make the road smooth. While we wait for this to happen we sink deeper into the mind set of thinking everything is impossible.

When we moved to our first home in the country we lived for 6 months without running water. It was tough with three small children: but we did it. The biggest obstacle I faced was my own pride and sense of injustice that this was happening to me. Oh well, it did happen and it was time for me to grow up and start thinking about how I had got to that place and how I was going to make the best of the situation.

Thank God we live in America.

I had to realize that there were people who were willing to help but that they were not going to do it for me. How many disappointments did I go through before I realized that? The government was not going to do it for me, my family was not going to do it for me, and nobody or business owed me anything. The one thing that really gets me is, the lotto is not going to do it for me. The first time I had to dig out my own septic tank all these things became very clear. If I was going to get something done I just had to get in there and get down right dirty.

When did we all forget this along the way?

THE FRUIT OF OUR LABOR

Every year I prune the apple trees. Fruit bearing branches are trimmed back. Branches too close together are taken out. Each and every twig and branch is looked at and trimmed in one way or another once a decision is made. If I let it go for a year the work is so much harder because the branches that need to be trimmed are much bigger around. Usually because of time constraints and energy levels I can't trim them all at once. I just do a little at a time, step back and look at it, then go at it again a couple days later. The whole process usually lasts a month. Most of the time I am actually up in the tree stepping out on the branches and working my way out as far as I can until the branch feels shakier than I feel comfortable with. I really feel like a monkey while I'm doing it. The rest of the time I am on a ladder. Often on the top step on tiptoe. I am very careful and have never fallen but each year I know that it is a possibility.

So what does that have to do with finances? Everything. Over the next few months you will be looking at every expenditure, every check written, to see what can be and needs to be trimmed back. If this has not been done in a long time it will take a bigger effort and you may have to call on some professional to help. Before you take action you need to study to do it correctly so that in the spring the tree will come back full and produce plentiful fruit. If you trim back too radically it will take longer to bear fruit, if you don't trim enough the tree will be weak and the fruit measly. Pruning is really art coupled with function.

Over the years I have seen many things happen to trees at the hands of those who are taking care of them. Pruned back so far they die. Trimmed lopsided. Not trimmed enough and the branches will break off. Bad pruning year after year will kill the tree or at least stop the fruit.

The other similarity is that whether you are reckless or use extreme caution there is always the possibility that you may fall. There is no way around that possibility. Knowing that comes that strange almost paralyzing fear occasionally. Fear is such a strange thing. It can come upon you almost without warning and change your whole body chemistry. It grips you and you feel powerless to overcome it.

In times of financial concern this can and will happen. There is a lot of responsibility on your shoulders and you might have many that you love that are depending on you to make it right even if they are still in diapers and don't know how to express it. They are counting on you. And you're not feeling like you can even count on yourself. And you certainly can't count on the employer who just told you that you are no longer needed, or the spouse who walked out the door, or the illness or injury that caught you unawares.

Oh yeah, I know that feeling. And you will too at some point in time. The only thing that I can tell you is don't look down.

Let's go on with our example of the apple tree.

A tree can die from disease. If the tree is your finances we will equate that to any financial activity that can ultimately destroy your finances. These must be treated. Drugs, alcoholism, chronic compulsive spending, and any hobby that becomes excessive. These are just examples. You will have to look at your own situation to find yours. If you are married your spouse may have been telling you about it for years, you just haven't been listening. Maybe now would be the time to quietly admit they were right.

Roots not deep enough. It always amazes me to see huge trees that have been blow over by the wind because they did not have enough roots. With our finances that would be not having reserve. It is recommended by financial people that we keep 6 months to a years worth of bill money in the bank. If you've been living payday to payday for whatever reason then your tree has no roots.

Lack of water. A tree can put out numerous buds to make fruit but if the tree doesn't get enough water the fruit will be pitifully small. We will liken this to maintenance and finishing projects. We get so busy and try to spread ourselves so thin that often the things that we have start suffering from lack of maintenance or projects get half done or even almost done and just set aside.

Rest. Many people don't know that a fruit-producing tree needs rest. Every seven years they are to sit and rest to go through their annual cycle without interference. Finances are the same way. Investments often just have to sit to produce.

Old age. Even a tree can die of old age. Certain careers become obsolete. The moneymaking opportunities of past generations can dry up and be useless. Sports personalities are well aware of this but we must be also. Technology and lifestyles change. What was hot today may be passé tomorrow. We need to look at what we are doing and how we are doing it in relation to the trends to make sure that we will be able to make a living tomorrow.

Why all this talk about trees? Study them and you will see the balance needed for fruit production. The storms will come just like they do in our own lives. If we will spend our time and energy to take care of our financial tree it will make it through the storms.

THE BEST OF TIMES,
THE WORST OF TIMES

Over the years I have read countless books on money management. I have spent years crunching numbers. And I have spent years trying alternatives to making, managing, and spending money. I have not been afraid to take giant leaps away from security to try something new. I have been called a survivor, a pioneer, and eccentric. I have been an assistant Vice-President and Manager in banking making very good money and on my way up. I have walked away to an uncertain future because I felt my family needed me at home. I spent 5 years experimenting with different jobs just to see the world from different perspectives. I have been a waitress and seen the generosity and goodness in people and at the next table seen people who evidently would welcome back slavery. I have worked at McDonald's, which by the way was one of the best-run companies I have been at. I have worked manual labor, office labor, had good pay and minimum wage.

Why do I share this? There is an old saying "Don't judge a man until you have walked a mile in his shoes". I have worn many pairs of shoes in my life. Some were comfortable and some pinched my toes and some even made me limp. I have at times chosen near poverty to enable me to spend time with my family. I have given up the idea of security in favor of adventure.

Not everyone can do this. Not everyone would want to. But like the seasons of the year, we all have our favorite but we do have to find a way to get though the rest of the year.

If you are reading this book it is probably because you are going through uncertain times. You are walking a new road that you have never been on. You are able to acknowledge that some new ideas might help you out.

You will be a conqueror. A survivor. Not the kind who bitterly tells of the hard times they went through with a care drawn face. Rather, you can look toward the past and the future cheerfully knowing that good can come out of hardship. I would not have learned how to install a toilet if I could have hired someone to do it. Some of my best recipes came from scouring the cupboards when there was no money to buy food. And you will no longer be a wimp. It is amazing how many whiny wimpy adults there are who must drown their sorrows and face their lives with getting drunk. Oops. I forgot, it's a disease. I thought about having it a few times but decided not to. Or the solution to hardship and poverty for the current generation is violence. If you don't like your life or feel like you have been dealt a bum hand go out and beat someone up. Innocent or guilty the object of wrath doesn't really matter. The jails are too full to put you away anyway.

If you are reading this you probably are not that type of person. You are looking for ideas, answers, and are willing to do the work to get through whatever you are going through right now that has impacted your finances.

THE BEST INVESTMENT
TOILET PAPER

If you have ever been down to your last $5 than you know how important toilet paper can be. If you haven't, then you'll just have to take my word for it. If you have ever been out then you know that you don't want to be out again.

Sound too simple? Well it is. Often time we spend so much time thinking about all the big things of how to manage our money that we forget what it really takes to keep a home running.

If you were to make a list of what you buy at the grocery store you would probably find that you buy pretty much buy the same things, week after week, month after month, year after year. Knowing what these things are brings a tremendous opportunity for volume buying. We'll get to how much you can save in a minute.

A typical list of what a family would buy:

- Chicken
- Hamburger
- Canned Vegetables

- Soups
- Noodles
- Potatoes
- Hamburger
- Fruits and vegetables
- Dairy products
- Bathroom products – toilet paper, shampoo, tooth-paste, etc.
- Cleaning products

So how much do you spend on groceries now? $300 per month? $500 per month? You don't know?

What if you could spend half of that? What if you could get by on $20 this month? Would that help out with the other bills or investments or goals?

I was never a good saver at the bank. No matter what I set aside it got spent somehow. So I had to look for some other way to save. And I found that food was the most flexible of all the budget items. No one was going to turn off your service or turn you into a collection agent if you didn't spend as much this month. And whatever I didn't use now I could use later.

I was actually on food stamps when I started this. I only had money for food once a month and it all had to be spent on food and nothing else. If I used them wisely they got us through the month, if I didn't we went without. And the amount they gave me was far less than I used to spend and more than I sometimes had been able to spend before.

So here we go, this is what I did. I took 10% of what I had to spend and called it my "Stocking Money". Having a name for it helped me make sure it got spent that way. I made my regular grocery list with the remaining 90%. With my stocking money I found the 2 best deals in the store of things we normally used. One time it might be canned food, one time it might be coffee, one time chicken. You get the idea. I used my stocking money to buy as much as I possibly could of the sale item. Sometimes I could get 3 cases of canned vegetables, another time it might be 30 pounds of chicken, or 6 big cans of coffee. Each month I did this. With my 10% I had an accumulation of up to 30 cases of food and a full freezer.

After a few months I found that I could increase my stocking money from 10% up to 50% because I had so many commonly used items stored up. I always found that I needed to keep at least 25% for fresh items, milk, and sometimes bread.

Long after my food stamp days I kept this up. Because it works. I bought a freezer to be able to keep more meats, breads, butter, and frozen vegetables in storage.

The biggest reason I have heard for not storing food is space. I had some shelves made but if what if you don't have room for them. What have you got under your bed? Under your stairs? The bottom of your kids closet? Your garage? If you look all around and still don't have the space then you might be interested in reading the next chapter about the 50% rule.

Some of the other benefits of food storage:

1. You can help your friends and family if they become sick or unemployed.

2. Company is no problem. You can feed an army.

3. If an unexpected or unplanned expense comes up you can use your food money and eat from the stored food. It isn't as fun as going to the store but at least your property taxes will be paid on time or you can get that broken leg fixed.

4. You will be surprised at how much less you worry about money even if you become unemployed. At least you know that your family can eat.

5. You can cut you food bill in half over the next few months.

Some other things I have found:

1. Most generic cleaning products and detergents just don't work as well as the name brands. Better to buy the name brand on sale than try a substitute.

2. Food Outlet stores are a great place for saving money. Sometimes the labels are in foreign languages but corn is corn once you get into the can.

3. Margarine, butter, and many cheeses can be frozen.

4. Storage times must coincide with how often you use the product. No one likes freezer burned chicken or stale cereal so know your storage time.

5. Store perishables like flour, sugar, noodles, etc in bug and mouse proof containers.

The library contains many good books on food storage if you would like more information than is provided here. Our purpose here is mainly to show how you can save money and actually create a investment program using food.

You know that you are rich when you have two cases of toilet paper on hand.

THE ANNUAL 50%

This will be fun, challenging, or almost impossible depending on your personality.

It is very easy to explain. Once a year go through every closet, every drawer, and every other storage area you have and try to get rid of 50% of everything you own. Sounds impossible but if you try it you will be shocked and surprised to find that you can actually do it. A friend and I did this together, we called ourselves essentialists.

I'm sure you're asking why you would even consider doing this. Very simply, most of us have far more than we need or use. As a result we keep on spending more money on more things that we don't need or use. Our houses get cluttered so we think we need a bigger house. Not only does it take money to buy, store, and maintain these items but it also takes time to buy, store and maintain these items.

The worst part about the whole situation is that if you go to sell these items, in most cases, and if you are lucky, you might get half of what you paid for it even if the item still has a price tag. At a garage sale the item often goes for pennies on the dollar. That, I think, is one of the main reasons we hate to get rid of extra stuff. We get internally outraged that no one wants to pay us "What it's really worth". So hidden in our closet we can keep on telling ourselves that it is hidden treasure and that we are lucky to have it.

The clothes closet is usually the easiest place to start with our 50% reduction. Usually it is easiest to start with someone else's clothes other than our own. Don't start with your spouse though. It can be a major issue if you get rid of their favorite shirt no matter how worn out or gross you think it is. So it's either your own clothes or your younger kids.

Take everything out of the closet. Everything. Now count how many pair of shoes you have. 20? 50? Okay. What is half? Go through and get whatever is never worn, worn out or just a weird color that you love but never wear. Throw it all in a box. And move through everything until the whole closet is done. There will be some very easy decisions and some very hard ones. There is a common rule that says to get rid of everything you haven't worn is a year. That works but for me some of the stuff I wear everyday is the stuff I most need to get rid of. Besides maybe you didn't wear it for a year because you completely forgot you had it.

After all of the sorting it is time to put away everything you have kept. Wow. How did the closet get so spacious? This is also a good time to reorganize how you keep things. Shirts together, slacks, and jackets. Everything neat and organized. I go so far as to color arrange everything like the rainbow and it looks great. Color and type organizing also helps you to notice that you still have 10 pairs of slacks and 3 shirts or a beautiful red blouse with nothing to go with it. I once noticed that almost everything I owned was black. If you do need to go shopping you have a better idea of what you really need.

The sock drawer is always great fun. Small children love to help you work on this one. After going through all the pairs of mismatched and holes in the heels you might find you only have three really good pairs. Or conversely, someone once gave me a big garage bag of socks that I washed and sorted and got about 60 good pairs of socks. I was able to give them to someone who needed them.

It is also a good time to add a new bar or shelf to your closet if needed.

Now, having successfully gone through 1 closet or 1 drawer what are you going to do with the stuff you have decided you don't need? Nothing. Just find a place to set it aside and out of the way for 3 months to 1 year. Sounds silly but a necessary part of the process. In two months you may find yourself digging through the box to get that winter scarf that you really shouldn't have gotten rid of.

Just as an experiment select a few items you are planning to get rid of. How much did the item cost? How much is it now worth if you were to sell it at a garage sale? How many times did you wear it? This might surprise you. Let's say you spend $100 on a dress you wore 4 times. That is $25 per each time you wore it. Now look at those favorite $7 sweatpants that you wore almost everyday after work and you are now getting rid of because they have been washed hundreds of times and are now an embarrassment.

So what is the point? The money spent is your investment dollars. Which item was the better investment? The question can be answered in two ways and it comes back to our needs, wants, and desires idea. The sweats were a much better investment from a usage standpoint so you might want to buy 3 more pairs just so they don't get so worn out. The dress was maybe a waste of money unless it helped you land your great job or attend your son's wedding. There is no right or wrong answer but by thinking about it you can make better decisions in the future.

After a few months have passed it's time to do something with all the stuff. If you haven't done so already, don't forget to dispose of the items that are stained, ripped, or otherwise unusable. You could have a garage sale. You could donate it to a thrift store. Or, you could take the items to your favorite charity. You can get a receipt for a tax-deductible contribution. My personal favorite is the pass around club, which I'll talk about in the next chapter.

I never finished answering the first question. Why would you want to do this?

1. Gives you more space for things you really do need or want to keep.

2. Someone else can use all the stuff you don't want or need. They may even be delighted.

3. I hate to mention this one but having lots of stuff attracts mice and other pests.

4. By going through all of your stuff you can learn a lot about your weaknesses and spending habits. Do you have a weakness for buying shoes? Do you buy clothes on sale that don't match anything else you own? Do you have clothes in your closet with price tags on? Or, do you love to buy fancy clothes that you never have anyplace to wear? Do you hate to mend and have many great clothes with missing buttons and hems coming out?

By taking the time to look at your spending habits you may come up with some better ways to use your money. This section has focused on clothes but the same methods and principles apply to all items in your house. Are your towels so worn out that they need to be replaced? Maybe having a garage sale will help you come up with the money to get some. Oh, and finally, check out the condition of your dishtowels and potholders. If you don't know what I'm talking about then good for you.

Toys, Toys, Toys.

A special note about toys. With all the birthdays and Christmas' that go by a child can end up with so many toys that they don't want to play with any of them. A couple quick tips. Get rid of all the broken ones. Designate a specific place where the toys are to be kept that limits the space available like a toy chest or a bookshelf. Pick out the favorite toys and box up the rest. Rotate the toys every couple of months. Kids love it when they get a fresh supply. But just make sure not to try and hide the favorite stuffed animal or doll. We are not trying to break any hearts here.

PASS IT ON

After doing my first essential 50% sorting I was ready to do something. Some items went to the thrift store but we happened upon a great alternative. I took all my bags to a friend's house and they sorted through, took what they wanted and passed it on. We continued the passing and friend after friend had a chance to go through it. They took what they wanted and added some more. Pretty soon we were passing everything from clothes, to drapes, to furniture. We all got blessed and it was surprising to find how often something we did not need was just the special thing that someone else needed and was glad to have. And we all were glad to get rid of stuff.

And that's all it is. You can be the one to start your own pass it on circle. Depending on what you have pick a person you think might be interested. No strings attached. That's the important part. Some people may take much and some just a little. Some may give much and some little. Don't worry about it. Remember these are things you don't want or need anyway.

If you don't have anyone to give them to you can check with the school to see if there is a needy family.

And, of course there are other ways to pass on your un-needed items.

- Thrift stores – Many will give tax-deductible receipts.
- Garage Sales.
- Advertise in the newspaper or at the grocery store bulletin board.
- Swap meets.
- Craigslist.

THAT NAGGING SENSE OF FEAR

During the time of financial downturn occasionally and sometimes without warning your stomach can get gripped with fear. I know whereof I speak. It happened to me just this morning.

We recently bought a new house. The old house was lined up to be rented. The numbers looked good. I have a great deal of equity in the first house so the rent I can get for the first house is enough to cover almost the full amount for both house payments. Great deal for us and still a good deal for the renter. A win/win transaction. I was using all the principles I recently acquired from real estate investment tapes and I could see how the whole plan would bring us closer to our short and long-term goals.

Then it happened. We had moved out of our old house into the new and I was madly trying to organize the new house and clean the old house. The renters were supposed to move in on Sunday and it was already Tuesday and we were living out of boxes with furniture piled all over the place because we needed to paint the entire inside of the house we had just moved into.

Tuesday evening arrives and I get a call from the renter with a ridiculous and lame excuse of why she won't be moving in. Two days later my employer advises me that due to low volume my hours would be cut from 40 per week to 16. When I applied for unemployment I found that I would have a one-week waiting period and then the amount I would get would be half of what I would have made.

So here I am with 2 mortgage payments, taxes and insurance are due and I'm working only two days a week and getting a small unemployment check.

Did I panic? No. I did have some reserve in the bank so I went ahead and made the October payment on both places. I began working on the old house and decided to sell it instead of renting it. I had planned to do it in the spring anyway because the renters had only wanted to stay for the winter and then move out of the state.

The old house is an hour away from the new house so I begin the treks back and forth taking one small load of the remaining stuff at a time. At least my two days a week give me more time to get things done.

We advertised and were able to find a buyer. But the delay of waiting for the lawyer to prepare the papers takes another two weeks. During this time many of the members of our family decide to visit to see our new house. I start looking for another job and start a class that should provide me another income source. Phone calls to get things taken care of have to be made four times to get anything done. My husband's family has major medical problems and the ex-wife decides its time for another round of whatever you want to call it that ex-wives do. Obstacles in time and money have depleted the reserves and put me behind schedule.

The clock ticks on and the month speeds by and it is almost time for another two mortgage payments.

I have looked and looked at the numbers. I have talked to all of the people who could impact the situation within the next couple of weeks. I have assured myself that everything should be okay and we are not behind.

But that knot in my gut is not listening to the logical thoughts I am feeding my brain. And why is that?

I think above all because I have left what I consider the safe and secure path I had been used to and when I thought I was steady on my feet someone else came along and gave me a shove. Such is life.

Change is hard. Or shall we say challenging to put it in a more positive way. We never quite know what is ahead and what might jump out from behind your careful planning. The adrenalin that it takes to get excited could be the same charge that makes you ready to jump out of the way at any minute.

So what can be done? Those times may come and go but the best idea I have found is to have a good plan with alternatives. A back up plan to the back up plan. When you know your are living on the edge it is scarier but the funny thing is that you already were on the edge. You just didn't realize it.

GET A JOB

As an apartment manager, which I do in addition to a full time job, running a ranch, and keeping up the house, I am increasingly concerned about the number of able bodied adults who would rather get behind on their bills than to look for a job.

Yes, the job market is tough. But, if you get up at 9:00 or 10:00 a.m., don't bother to shower or shave why would anyone ever want to hire you? Lazy. An old fashioned word that is very unpopular these days. Yes, I've heard about all the hard luck stories and how tough it is and how you just need a little help this month to get you by but it amazes me how a person can have too much pride to work a minimum wage job but not too proud to ask for an extension when the rent is due. I guess the only ones they are kidding is themselves and then get bitter because the help and patience of others runs out.

One thing I see: a hard worker will work and find something to do whether they get paid for it or not. A lazy person will find all the reasons why he just can't do it today.

What can you do if you are a hard worker and find yourself unemployed? What if you are a lazy person who is tired of being broke. Well, get to work. But "I don't have a job", you say. It doesn't matter, get to work. Wake early in the morning, shower, shave, and look around and you can find work to do wherever you turn. Is your yard immaculate? Is your house spotless? Is your car clean? Is your mom's house, yard, and car clean? Does the neighbor down the street need help with anything? Does the school need a volunteer to plant some flowers or read to children? Does the widow lady at church need her house painted or lawn mowed?

But why would you want to do any of these things for free? Here are some of the reasons:

1. You will get all those projects and tasks done that you don't have time to do while you are working. Many projects can be done for free or at minimal cost so you don't have to break the bank and your family will love you for getting the house, cars, and yard maintained.

2. You will meet new people in the community. Someone may hire you or refer you to someone who can.

3. Some will repay your work with what they have even if it is not cash. This is especially prevalent in farming communities where you could get a freezer full of meat or corn for a few days work.

4. You will be making a valuable contribution to individuals and organizations in your community.

5. You will be known to all as a roll up your sleeves and get in there kind of person. Employers look for this.

6. You will sleep better at night knowing that you have accomplished more than just watching Jerry Springer.

7. Did I say that others will see what a hard worker you are and may want to hire you?

Most of all, your dignity and self-respect will remain intact and it will show as you go look for jobs.

Right now, I have fences to paint, pens to build, and a room to get sheet-rocked. I have no cash. BUT, I have a freezer full of steak, hamburger, and roasts. I also have enough wood to heat a house for the winter. Bartering tools. The hard workers I know are too busy to take on anymore. And the others I wouldn't hire. And, it must be that no one else will either because they are still unemployed.

The moral to the story is clear. There is lots of work to be done. We need more hard workers to do it.

Oh, and of course, there are those who do a great job the first time and then you hire them back again and they start padding their hours, getting sloppy with their work, or not showing up when they say they will. Guess what? It only will happen once or twice and I will tell others who ask. Good and bad reputations do get passed around.

MOVING HOME

Look around. You will be surprised to find how many people have gone home. It has been a growing trend in the past 10 years. The most common time is the first year or so after a divorce. No one really talks about it much. As adults, few people want to admit that they are living with their parents. Yet it is happening more and more. The other trend that is growing is parents moving in with children.

I think the reason that this is becoming more common is because it works. Americans are relearning what many cultures have always known, the extended family helps all. When a person is broken or beat up emotionally or financially home is a good place to go. And the recovery is amazingly quick. Much quicker than trying to do it on your own. Why? Because you are around people who care. And the economics of shared housing allow for a rapid financial recovery.

In my observation after the initial feelings of chagrin at moving home all parties involved really do smile a lot more. Grandchildren love the attention. Retired moms seem to be rejuvenated at having someone to "mother" again and though they gripe sometimes they often help with the childcare which provides added economic and security benefits. More importantly the interaction gives all persons involved a sense of belonging.

Or course there is the downside. Old differences may arise between parents and their adult children. I know a man close to 40 who had to move to his parents' home to recover from a car accident. At midnight the doors got locked whether he was home or not. There are often arguments about phone usage, who will mow the lawn, or how much to contribute for food. The big issue is often control. Parents who used the adage that "this is my house and you will do what I say" have a hard time giving this up even though their children are grown and may have their own children. Grown children sometimes take a step back and become less responsible than they would be on their own.

But the bottom line is that this is family. And whether the temporary move home lasts three months or five years, or, in some rare situations becomes a permanent life time move it can be a great advantage emotionally and financially to all parties. There may be some misunderstandings at times but that is also part of being family.

It is wonderful to be loved and love is the greatest riches that life has to offer.

IT'S ONLY TEMPORARY - PART 1

Hopefully, you're right.

Whenever I have been unemployed or had a salary reduction, even if it is only for three months, it takes almost a year to get back where I was.

It's happened a couple of times so I have been able to figure out why it takes so long.

1. First, since I tell myself it is only temporary I don't make the changes to my spending that I need to early enough. So my spending is at a much higher rate than my income.

2. As a result, my reserves end up being depleted. The longer things go on the less flexibility I have to recover.

3. Third, it's so nice to have time off that I try and catch up on everything I was behind on. This includes social visits with friends, house cleaning, and making cookies. The only problem with this approach is that I am not spending enough of my time doing those things that may result in an income.

4. Fourth, the time always ends up being longer than I expect, the competition is tougher, and though I expect to be able to find a job easily there were lots of other people also getting laid off. A number of times I have been told that up to one hundred applicants have responded to one advertisement in the paper.

5. Next, unemployment, if you are able to get it, has waiting weeks with no check. When a check does arrive it is about half of my old income. So I start out behind and have to play catch-up and it gets very stressful. Money worries absorb much of my thinking from the time I wake up, throughout the day, and even while sleeping. It is hard to be enthusiastic and positive while this is my mental state.

6. Next, maintenance on cars, the house, routine medical appointments, and priorities all get behind and it takes time and money to get them caught up again.

7. Finally, when I do get a new job it often starts out less than the salary I left behind. At least for the first few months.

So, knowing all this, what can be done?

Just the opposite of what I have done in the past.

1. Expect that you will need to be on minimum spending habits for at least a year and make the adjustments immediately.

2. If you have more cars than you need, sell them. This will give you cash for bills and decrease your expenses. Don't forget to call you auto insurance provider.

3. Be very stingy with reserves. If there is plenty, it might be a good time to review other investments but make sure to keep enough cash available for bills and expenses.

4. Immediately consider the search for a job or other income sources as your primary job.

5. Consult temporary agencies and consider lots of job avenues that you may not have considered in the past.

6. Hang in for the long haul and don't get discouraged.

7. Be thankful for all that you have. Develop an attitude of gratitude for the things that you have and the things you took for granted.

8. Remember that better days have been here before and they will come again.

IT'S ONLY TEMPORARY - PART 2

Often when we have times of good fortune we tend to think that the good times are here to stay. When we get a raise at our job we think that it is just the next step and we anticipate and expect that we will get another raise next year. We believe this because we want it to be true. We want to believe that all hardship is in the past and we have conquered, overcome, and achieved, and will continue to do so.

Unfortunately this is not always true except for a small few and not for those living in these days of rapid change. Just as the hard times will pass, so will the good times.

While the good times are here it is good to enjoy the new experiences, and catching up on the needs, wants, and desires that we have long put on hold and patiently waited for. But while doing so we would also be wise to realize that these times somehow, some way, will pass.

Somehow we need to expect this and use our peak times to prepare for the days of famine in the land. By famine I refer to times of unemployment, bad health, or conflicting needs. These can happen within our own family or to those we love and care for such as parents, grown children, and close friends.

Somehow at all times we must be prepared to lose the bulk of our income for even up to a year at a time.

How much do you have in savings?

How much food do you have stored for your use?

Do you have life insurance to cover the amount of your outstanding debts?

Are the things you own well maintained so that if necessary you would not have to spend anything for the next year?

No one can prepare for all circumstances. Trouble seems to come in the back door. And we can't constantly worry that they will come. But they will. For a short time, a long time, or anywhere in between.

I once read that 98% of all Americans are within 90 days of homelessness. Put another way – only 2% of Americans own their own home completely. I speculate that most of these are over age 65 and unfortunately with the new option of the reverse mortgage these could dwindle away also.

We live in the age of debt and mortgage. Most of us may never get out in our lifetimes. All the more critical is the need to have a reserve. At least a reserve to cover our food and debt payments for a few months. The bills will keep coming. Our paycheck may not.

IF SHOPPING IS YOUR PASSION THEN GET ANOTHER HOBBY

There's one thing we can agree on. Shopping costs money. Even if you go out with the best of intentions, a list, and a maximum limit it is oh so easy to spend more. As you bring home all your treasures and put them away the sense of accomplishment almost out shouts the small feeling that you spent more than you should have.

I for one am not much of a shopper but every few years I can go out and spend thousands. I guess I save up my shopping tendency and have occasional blowouts where I lose it and buy all the things I have thought of for the last 10 years.

Even though I am not a regular shopper I have known many people who are and these are my conclusions after many years of observation. Maybe you will see yourself and having once done so you can develop a plan for cutting down.

Shopping is a social event. Malls are one of the few places that still welcome children and they don't even have to behave well. As long as they think that you might spend money they invite you to come on in. Friends are also welcome. Just make a phone call and your best friend can join you for an evening of fun. And best of all, you can get all dressed up or come as you are.

Regain your power. This sounds strange but I have seen it often. A break up with a boyfriend. A job lay-off. Even the rumor of a lay-off. All of these things make a person feel like they have lost some of the power over their lives. It causes a person to realize that despite all that we hear about taking charge of our lives there are some things outside of our control and the people who have control don't always treat us the way we want or deserve to be treated. But since we cannot always change these events we shop to take charge of our lives and soothe our bruised or broken ego. Sometimes this is okay. A new haircut, a workout program at the gym, a new wardrobe, all of these things are good for us and maybe we should have done it long ago. But we can't ignore the financial impact it has, especially if we pull out the charge card to do it. If we do come home and haven't spent anything we can still pat ourselves on the back because we have held on to our money and we can tell ourselves that we exercised self-discipline.

Compensate for our inability to achieve the other things. When we feel like or know that we can't afford the more expensive things we need or want we try to compensate by finding something we like and get that instead to try and cover our feelings of hopelessness. An extreme example is those who live in deplorable housing conditions but have a beautiful new car. They feel they can't afford to make a $1,500 month house payment but they can pay a $500 per month car payment. They drive the car proudly to show to themselves and the world that they are somebody. But that is the extreme. Maybe you can't relate. How about when you can't afford the house of your dreams so you lavish your apartment with dynamite furnishings? Getting closer? Or, how about the bills are too high so you go to a restaurant or the grocery store and find the best steak you can't really afford? This last example is probably the most common because it is so easy to rationalize. But the more often you indulge this feeling the farther you will be from your long-term goals. Why is it indulgent? Because it is a substitute for your bigger goals and is out of balance with your overall financial situation.

Boredom. Shopping provides some instant gratification and is a lot easier than sitting home every Friday night.

Laziness. Sounds terrible and if this is you you'll be tempted to say it's not. But maybe after consideration you can name someone who falls in this category. Shopping really doesn't require much creativity. The stores have worked hard to coordinate all the clothing, linens, and even the make-up. But the trick is that it is set up so that we feel creative as we pick up all the items and put them together. Another form of laziness is that most people I know that are avid shoppers don't have any or few other interests that they pursue.

Whether it is calligraphy, reading, sewing, or scuba diving, all of these things take effort and time to study and become good at. Shopping is easy. All you have to do is look, pick, and pull out your wallet.

Creativity. I know that I said that little creativity is involved but by the same token it can be extremely creative to shop 100 stores just to find the exact right piece of furniture to go in that empty corner of the living room. So it is just as valid to say that people use shopping to explore and fulfill their creativity.

To relieve tension. There are times when shopping can be a mental and emotional release from the problems and day to day routines we all have. A time to just look around. To remember our dreams and goals. A time to make some new goals and figure out what we will do with that awful kitchen. Even if our dream kitchen never comes to reality it was good just to have dreamed it and refreshes us to go back home to do the dishes.

These are the biggest reasons I have observed why people shop. None of them are bad. But in order to reach our financial goals we have to look at how we spend our money and decide if we are maximizing our assets, time, and resources.

If we want to cut down our spending or maximize our dollars we have to see why we are shopping and try to fulfill those emotional needs within our budget. But why now refer to them as emotional needs? Didn't you notice how often I used the word "feel" when referring to why we shop. The word feel indicates that it is our emotions and not our actual physical needs or logic that drive us to the mall. That is why so often we have things that we hardly use, don't need, and wonder why we bought it in the first place. The bright pink blouse that matches nothing – we needed to feel cheerful. The black dress we have worn twice? We may have felt bad and the dress expressed our feelings at the time. Or the jazzy party dress? We wish we went out more. These are just speculations but it is easy to see how we can buy things to express how we feel, compensate for how we feel, or show how we want to feel or who we wish we were. I have a pair of new ballet shoes that I bought, took one lesson, but can't seem to get rid of because it would be really cool to be a ballerina. Go ahead and laugh then check your own closets and see what strange and wonderful things you have hidden away.

The reasons people are passionate about shopping are many. But there is one solution that applies to all: Get a hobby. The word itself is almost obsolete and comes from past generations. Therefore, we have to look to past generations to get some ideas of what a good hobby might be. The one criteria required for our purpose is that the hobby must require more time than money. Many modern day activities involve more money than time. The reason is simple. We are introduced to them by the companies selling the pieces, parts, and equipment to perform the hobby. Even Christmas now is primarily promoted by the stores.

Below are some ideas for lower cost hobbies. If they are totally new then consider it an adventure to shop for a hobby. Try them all on to see how they fit before deciding it's not for you. Also, remember that many of these involve acquiring a skill. At first it will take some work and mistakes and maybe frustration before you get the hang of it. You probably won't be good at it at first. Start with a minimum investment and set yourself a limit you can afford before you go hobby shopping. You don't want a lot of half finished projects around the house but on the other hand if you spend $20 on your new test hobby and spend weeks of evenings at home before you decide you hate it and toss it aside you still have probably saved a lot of money by not going shopping.

So here are the ideas:

1. Read to your children. Let them read to you.
2. Embroidery.
3. Learn to play bridge and teach your best friends.
4. Knitting.
5. Yard work.
6. Crochet.
7. Play board games.

8. Paint-by-the-number. (You don't have to create a masterpiece. Just have fun.)
9. Models.
10. Make doll clothes from scrap material.
11. Walk and keep track of how far you walk.
12. Bird Watching. Get a book and mark and date the ones you see.
13. Needlepoint.
14. Cooking.
15. 1000 piece puzzles.
16. Learn to play chess.
17. Take dance lessons.
18. Fishing.

The local community centers and senior centers have many low cost classes. For about $25 you can get an introduction to a whole new craft, skill, or activity. Through adventure and experimentation you may find a whole new outlet for your individuality and buried creativity. The diamond in the rough in this case is you.

IF KIDS WERE MEANT TO FLY

The easiest way to tell the story is to tell you about Joe and Michael.

Joe couldn't wait to grow up. His parents told him that they would buy him a car when he was 16. He counted the days.

Finally it happened. A new car, insurance paid for, and they even kicked in some gas money. Joe spent the next two years hanging out with his friends waiting for the next milestone in his life, which was when he turned 18 and moved out. Right after high school he got a job and was ready to make the move. Now that he had his own place he could have girls over and someone was always able to get some beer or whatever sounded good. It was one big party all the time. If he ran short on food or the rent some of his friends would pitch in because they were often over and crashed on the couch. By age 22, Joe had racked up credit card bills to the limit, had his car half way paid off, and no extra money in the bank. He met Candy and she started spending the night on a regular basis. When they found out she was pregnant she moved in permanently. They were so excited to have a baby coming along. The doctor said it was going to be a boy.

This is not a real person but a composite of many people I have met. Young adults who go off into the world unprepared, unskilled, and headed for trouble and headaches the rest of their lives. Is it surprising then that under the stress of this that the divorce rate soars and everyone is left for the worse for years to come? It may take until they are thirty or forty to recover and get back on track.

The next story is a true one of my own son Michael. I homeschooled Michael in the forth grade because I wanted to ensure that he got a good start. We did everything together. Unit pricing at the grocery store, working business deals, hammering nails, and managing the house. I would have him prepare a menu for a month, make a grocery list and off we would go shopping. His first business was raising rabbits. We worked to figure the expenses and we worked with a rabbit farmer in trade for the cages. We worked together to build the big shed that was to house the cages. He saved his money to get his first rabbits and we did all the paperwork to plan and manage his business and look at the profitability. The rabbit business ultimately did not make a profit and we sold the rabbits but we did succeed because he retained all these lessons.

At this time I began talking to him about a wife. Yes, a forth grader. I told him that someday he would want to marry but that he had to prepare so that he could provide for a wife. I told him it was the man's job to provide the house and that he shouldn't even start dating until he had a house because he might fall in love and he would not be ready and have nothing to offer. I reinforced these ideas over the years and although he didn't do things exactly as I said, (what kid does?), he was listening.

As far as traditional structured school work we spent two hours a day in studies and incorporated the rest into our daily activities. He learned his fractions while we cooked and baked. From this he started a pie baking business. We studied Spanish and worked on memorizing the Declaration of Independence. When he took his required annual state tests he scored in the tenth to 12th grade level on all subjects.

The next two years he attended private school on a scholar-ship for low-income people. I was required to provide the transportation so I worked at McDonalds because it was the only job that would work with my schedule.

Don't think we were rich during this time. I was a single mother of three children. My mother helped with the mort-gage payment and economy and thrift was our way of life.

When Michael was in the 8th grade we stayed at my mother's for almost a year. The older kids had already moved out. There were more job opportunities in the bigger city for me at that time and I worked one full time job and a part-time job. I continued to keep and pay for my own home in the rural community. My goal was to get out of debt and return home. After one year my financial situation greatly improved and I did move home. I also remarried.

Michael decided that he would like to stay at my mother's because he had already found a job with the city parks department and also an ice cream store. The decision was mutually agreeable to all so we did it. At age 16 he got a job at a bank as a teller under a training program. He worked full time in the summer and adjusted his school so he could work part-time while he finished high school and took a couple of early college classes. Don't think that he didn't have a social life. The weekends were go, go, go.

When he graduated he worked full time for the bank and joined the Army Reserve. All this time he stayed with my mother rent free and banked and invested all of his extra money.

At age 20, he bought his first house with two other guys with the plan that they would sell it in about 5 years. At age 21, he bought his first 4 unit apartment which I manage for him. At age 22, he is working on obtaining other investment properties. He is also getting serious about dating and is ready when he finds the right girl. He drives a Mercedes SUV. He is active duty in the army and is a Realtor with whatever extra time he can make.

The point of this long story I hope is clear. There is a different road. We don't have to wait until they are 18 and boot them out to sink or swim. We can equip and prepare them for the inevitable task of providing for themselves and choosing a spouse. These things don't just happen by magic.

We can teach them as much as we can and then hope and pray that they will use the tools we give them wisely. And, when I say hope and pray I do mean it literally.

HAIRCUTS FOR
THE WHOLE FAMILY

With 4 people in the family haircuts can get expensive. So early in my children's lives I decided to cut their hair. I went to the library and studied the how to cut hair book. I bought the clipper and scissors kit at Kmart and set out to work. I figured that by the time they were old enough to care that I would get good at it. I had time to practice.

I had the very curly haired boy, the straight haired boy, and the massive haired daughter. I must say that the curly haired boy was always the easiest. We even got creative with short on the sides and long on the top. The thing that was great about his hair was that any mistake could be covered by simply patting the hair down. The straight haired boy was definitely harder. You could see the mistakes but I worked at it until it was acceptable. With my daughter, I confess, I did make an unforgivable mistake of cutting her bangs too short one time. To this day, 20 years later she will not allow her bangs or her daughter's bangs to be cut. I feel guilty that I have warped her for life. But I have continued to practice on my own bangs and have gotten pretty good.

When the kids were about 14 or so they started cutting each other's hair. At one point my oldest son was cutting the hair of 5 kids at school. One time I came home and these were a bunch of his friends lined up and waiting so he must have been pretty good. Then the shave it off time came and no holds were barred and everyone got a turn and had a great time at it.

I still cut my husband's hair occasionally and do a pretty good job. But, as he always says "the difference between a good haircut and a bad one is about two weeks." My son cuts his kid's hair and my daughter still has her phobias about bangs.

Nothing ventured, nothing gained. We all have many ways to save money if we are courageous and adventurous enough to try it.

THE PRICE OF A HORSE

There are many things I learned to do right with finances and a few that I clearly did not and ended up regretting later.

There comes a time in every kid's life that they feel a passion to pursue something. For my daughter it was a horse and it came when she was around 12. For someone else it could have been basketball, skiing, a musical instrument, or watching the stars. For her it was a horse.

I'm not talking about the pursuit of always wanting to have the newest style in clothes or the newest video game. I'm talking about passion. The passion that shows who they really are as individuals.

At the time I felt, in fact, I knew, that we couldn't afford it. And the mistake I made was that I didn't try hard enough. I thought someday would be soon enough. But it wasn't. She had some friends who had a horse that she spent more and more time with. Less and less with me. You see, her love for horses was a way to express her individuality, with or without me.

As the years passed she, like most teenagers, spent lots of time with her friends. They didn't have horses. They choose rather to smoke, drink, and skip school which they did all their high school years. Later she moved out of town, hundreds of miles away.

It took about 10 years after the time that she first wanted a horse that I was finally able to get one. I thought she would be excited but by then she already had her own life and in fact had grown afraid of horses.

The moral of the story is sometimes for our kids we just have to work it out. We have to make sure we leave no room for regret and "what if". I miss her a lot and wished she lived close enough that we could ride horses together. My daughter did turn out great and gave up the party days to raise a family so now I am starting to work on my granddaughter. I hope to impart to her my love of horses so she will want to stay with us for the summers. By then I wonder if I will still be able to get up on one.

BICYCLE BUILT FOR TWO

The most important thing about cutting expenses whether you are doing it by choice or necessity is to always maintain a sense of creativity and a sense of humor.

When we first got married finances were really tight. We could barely make it from payday to payday and the gas tank always ran out with about a week before my next check. But since I had a job I would leave an hour early and walk the three miles to work. I encouraged myself by telling myself how good it was for my health and I certainly didn't want to be complaining to others about how hard of a time we were having.

One day as I started home I saw my husband parked on his bike in town. He waved me over and told me to get on. Because I always wore a dress to work it had to be sidesaddle. We took off down the road after some initial wobbling as he tried to keep his balance and headed the two miles remaining to home. We talked and laughed and had a great time. All the neighbors who passed in their cars laughed, smiled, and waved.

Each day after that my friend at work drove me to town. Jerry would be at the corner to meet me and off we would head toward home. We became the talk of the town and Jerry actually got to be a pretty popular guy because he always made people smile.

Then the paycheck would come and we would fill up the tank and drive until the money ran out again. This went on for a couple of months and it was one of the brokest (this is not really a word but it should be) times we have ever had. But we had some good times and good memories.

When you're broke it is so easy to worry, complain, and wish for better days. These can be the better days if we just allow ourselves to not take it all so seriously. We have money for gas now but every so often my husband still runs out because he forgets to check the gauge.

Just smile and use your creativity.

PANHANDLING FOR STAMPS

We have been trying to save money for so long it is almost a game. When we moved to our new house the local grocery store had a program of giving away stamps for every $5 purchase. The stamps go on little cards that hold six stamps per card. When the card is full you can get free and discount items. Each week is a different series of about 5 choices.

My husband and I are both old enough to remember when our parents used to get green stamps at the grocery and gas stations. So we loved the idea of being able to get all the cool stuff. It's so much more fun when you can buy something for 10 cents or better yet, for free.

So we both diligently save our stamps. Thanksgiving was coming up and with 65 stamps we could get our turkey for 19 cents a pound. (This is 2002 so you know that is a great deal). But as the time grew near we were 11 stamps short to be able to get our turkey.

We scoured the house, the drawers, and my purse but we couldn't come up with any more stamps.

I have to tell you about my husband here: he's not shy. In fact he loves to chat with people and can spend the whole day just visiting with friends and strangers alike. He was so well liked in our old town that he was told that he was the most popular guy in town. Everyone in town knows more about our business than I really wish they would. But guess who tells them?

Back to the story. It is three days before Thanksgiving and we really need to get that turkey so it can start defrosting. We were also out of coffee so my husband sets off for the store to get it. He came home with coffee, a turkey, and a big grin on his face.

"I panhandled for stamps," he says. As happy as can be he tells me how he waited outside the door and asked people if they wanted their stamps. In no time at all he had his 11 stamps and his $4 turkey.

Now I know most people wouldn't do this. I wouldn't. But my husband would. And somehow through it all he'll become the most popular guy in this town too. Amazing how far a smile can go.

BETTER NOT BITTER

The kids are all grown and when we are able to get together for holidays the "remember when…." stories always start as we sit around the table. And then the game begins. It always starts when someone says "You know you're poor when….." And the stories go on and on. By the end we are laughing to tears and our sides are splitting. Somehow through it all we have been able to get past the hard times and find laughter in them.

I have met many that are not so fortunate. When the times of hardship come up their whole face changes. They have difficulty talking about it and when they do their face reflects either fear or bitterness. Each of their stories is slanted to the why me, and poor me tone. But the stories that they tell are almost the same.

I realize that there are truly times when lack of money can cause some terrible outcomes. This is especially true of not being able to have adequate medical care resulting in pain, disfigurement, and sometimes even death. These are not things to laugh about.

But for the most part the effect is short lived and the thing that hurts the most is our pride. Even when we go through hard times the sun still rises in the morning and spring comes each year so we have reason to be thankful.

Even those who exuberate bitterness can tell stories of great creativity, ingenuity, and personal strength yet the beauty and courage of the story is clouded by the sneer on their faces while they tell it. If this is the way they remember things how then must it be affecting their current choices and decisions. Security and having what they missed becomes extremely important. In some ways they set a great example by making sure that they have enough in the bank and don't take any risks. They make sure that their kids have what they lacked. These are great and noble things and I have found that these people can give great advice for financial planning and economizing and I go to them often for advice.

But how much better if the frown could be replaced with a smile. And there is much to smile about. We made it through the hard times. We have learned much from the choices and challenges we faced. And if we are wiser now we have paid the price for our wisdom so it is ours to keep.

Maybe we have experienced much disappointment. But through it we have learned what we can count on and what we can't so we don't have to make the same mistakes again. People may have let you down but have we learned how to not let others down or have we adopted an every man for himself attitude?

There is an old saying that necessity is the mother of invention. During times of hardship we can look at what is really important without all the frills and focus to stabilize and improve these things.

For me it has been family teamwork and unity. As we worked though our challenges together we grew better, not bitter.

GET A GREAT DEAL ON A HOUSE

How would it change your life if your house were paid off? What if you had a chance to get completely out of debt? How much could you live on? If you have done your homework and prepared the Minimum Basic Budget you can easily answer these questions.

It is a well kept secret that the farther you get from the city the more house you can get for your money. Why is it a secret? A couple of reasons come to mind. First, there are far more city dwellers than those that live in the country. Second, country dwellers are hesitant about newcomers so they don't advertise. City dwellers are different than country dwellers. We are much more aware of the difference than you are. I too moved from the city years ago and am now able to see both sides.

But here are the numbers. Our house cost $150,000. It is a good-sized 3-bedroom rambler, 14 acres, horse stables, round pen, hot tub, and many other features. It is in average condition. This same house if moved 40 miles closer to Interstate 5 could be sold for $250,000. If it was located closer to Seattle it could be sold for about $550,000.

Or let's look at it in reverse. My friends own a home in south Seattle that they just sold for $179,000. The same house down here would go for about $75,000.

And if we lived even farther out the deals would get even better. The farther away you are from major population areas the more house you can get for your money.

Who might want to consider a move to the country?

1. Those with no job or prospects for employment.

2. Those with equity in their home.

3. Those with "needed" skills. Medical professionals, teachers, mechanics, plumbers, etc. Even in small towns there is a need for these professions. The salary is lower but so is the cost of living.

4. Those with regular income not subject to employment. Social security, disability, retirement pensions.

5. Those who are sick and tired of the rat race.

6. Those who love animals, working outside, or other activities associated with country life.

7. Those who like to do things with their own hands.

8. Those with their own business not required to be close to the city.

9. Writers, Artists, other independent professions.

10. Those who always wanted to live a simpler life and take more responsibility for the outcome of their choices.

Moving out of the city is not for everyone. But sometimes if all the roads seem to lead to dead ends it's time to look for new opportunities. The current popular expression is "Living outside the box". Well, when are you going to try it?

One last note. If you have access to a computer you have access to most newspapers in the whole country. So you can check out the prices, employment opportunities, and weather conditions without leaving your home (or the library).

THE FIXER HOUSE

Sometimes what we think is the worst thing that can happen ends up being one of the best. This is what happened to me with my first fixer. If you are considering a fixer or have considered a fixer let me tell you how bad this one was.

I was no longer working because I had quit to take care of my father who was terminally ill. My ex husband was not working because he had gotten himself with some bad company and bad habits (that's all I'll say about that). Our finances had gone steadily and rapidly downhill. They had gotten so bad that I saw no way to turn back. The house was close to foreclosure and since it was an owner contract and not a bank loan the owner allowed me to sign the house back to him. We lost our home and all the equity but didn't have our credit rating destroyed.

My ex and I went to the small town 100 miles away that my dad grew up in to try and find a place to live. To this day I have no idea why he thought of going from the large city of Seattle to the small town of Winlock, population 1000. We spent all day looking at run down old places and found a place that was vacant and built at the turn of the century. The realtor told us that we could lease to own it and decide whether we wanted to buy in a year.

Our payments were $200 per month for the first year. That sounds wonderful until you consider that we were city folks. The house had not been lived in for at least 5 years. There were broken windows, broken doors, a sagging floor, no heat source, and no running water. The house was listed as uninhabitable right on the contract. It came with 16 acres of land. It did have electricity. We decided to take it. We had no other options that we could see.

Then things got worse.

My ex and I made another trip down to clean the place up. We threw out an old mattresses that made me want to throw up. The living room had 3 layers of old area rugs which we took out and burned along with the drapes that were so greasy that it made your skin crawl just to touch them. We cleaned and cleaned.

Now came moving day. We packed up our possessions from our 4 bedroom, 2,500 square foot house. With the help of his brothers we got the truck all loaded up and ready to move out. Then the phone rang. My ex said he had to leave to meet some of his friends and that he would be back in three days. We were to go ahead and he would meet us there. So we took off and I cried the whole 100 miles.

The days came and went and my ex did not return. I had no way to even get a hold of him to see what was going on. It was the beginning of October and winter was coming in fast. The rain came down everyday for a month for that first winter and then it got cold.

No running water was the first of our challenges. We borrowed water in 5 gallon containers for bathing and cooking. We had to improvise on making a toilet. Seeing no way around it I got on welfare. With the first check I was able to purchase a wood stove for the living room and a relative gave us some wood. We were roughing it in ways I had never considered. The wind blew in through my broken bedroom window and the nights were very cold and got even colder. The stove did not have a proper draft and was almost useless for keeping the house warm.

At one point that winter I had to send the kids off to a relative's home to sleep and stay warm. I did what I could to keep the house from totally freezing. I remember we had ice that year inside and outside of our windows and the temperature got down to 14 degrees outside and about 35 in the house. At one point I laid on the couch and cried to the Lord "If this is my life than just take it". The answer I got was surprising. I knew that I was supposed to praise God and be thankful for all the good things. At first I couldn't do it but with tears streaming down my face I started singing "Great is Thy faithfulness".

Within days of these events the weather warmed up and we were given a free round trip visit to Hawaii. All expenses paid. I'm not kidding. When we returned home the weather had warmed up.

My ex helped by giving the money for the down payment for the house and some other repairs but he never did return home. We were on our own. During those early years we struggled and began to actually make improvements to ourselves, our lives, and our house. We had some help from friends for which I will always be thankful. We learned how to make the best of situations and gained important skills like how to replace a toilet.

THE FIXER-UPPER

COUNTING PENNIES

I used to keep two big jars that I filled with pennies. After years of collecting I had thousands and thousands of pennies. There came a time when that was the only money we had in the house. I remember it was wintertime. The evenings were long and dark.

My three children and I sat on the living room floor and counted and rolled pennies on many evenings. This would give us enough for bread, or a few groceries to get us by.

Sounds pitiful doesn't it. But it was fun. We talked and laughed and told stories. We were and still are a close family. Probably in part because of the long hours we spent rolling pennies.

I guess there are two morals to the story:

1. Enjoy every moment you have with your family.

2. Save your pennies. You might need them.

YOU'LL GET PAID WHEN I DO

So far in my adult life no one has offered to pay me to do my own housekeeping, the laundry, or wash my car. I keep asking but so far no takers. What's worse yet is that most of the time I am cleaning someone else's mess and not my own.

So why do we pay our kids to do these things and call it an allowance. What's worse is that we have to nag them and remind them to do it and often have to finish it up to do it right.

Here's another angle. We all live here, and we all work. We all eat here, so we work. We all sleep here, so we work. Sound harsh? Practice it out loud until you can say it confidently to your five year old or your fifteen year old.

Well, you ask, how are they going to learn how to handle money? Easy, once they have been trained at home they can go to the neighbors and offer their services to neighbors and have all the skills to do it right. A kid who can mow lawns and clean flowerbeds at 14 can have his own landscaping business at age 18. If he doesn't want to do the work he can hire the next up and coming 14 year old. A person that can clean house well can make far more money than the same person who goes and gets a job at a fast food restaurant. And can set their own hours after school, weekends, and college. If you don't know how much a housekeeper makes just look in the phone book, make a few calls, and you might be tempted to quit your job and start your own business.

It is well known that service jobs are high in demand and will be for years to come. We have all the tools we need at home to be teachers. I know that we all don't want our kids to be in the service industry. We have bigger plans, like college. Great. All the better. But we can still teach our kids to work, to strive for excellence, and best of all to start their own businesses.

"Inspection time." That's what my kids always heard after our weekend cleaning assignments. I would go in look under beds, check all corners, closets, and make sure the sheets were straight. Anything not done right was done again. I still remember their faces as they waited and watched me inspect. They beamed with pride when it passed. There was no arguing or negotiating or procrastinating for they knew I was the "Inspector" and it had to meet my standards, not theirs. Did they get money? No. Did they get treats or more TV? No. They got a sense of accomplishment at a job well done.

Our family has a joke. When the 2 boys got home from boot camp they both said it was a breeze after living with me. They also said that they couldn't believe how many grown men were getting in trouble because they couldn't make a bed, dress themselves neatly, or pick up their clothes. Grown men would cry because they couldn't pass inspection.

Teaching and training our kids to work hard, strive for excellence, and contribute to a family is one of the greatest gifts we can give them. The skills and discipline will put them in good standing in whatever field or vocation they choose. And the best thing is that one person won't be sitting and watching TV while the other scrambles around to get everything done. (Know what I mean?)

So when do we start? Well my four year old granddaughter helped me start the dishwasher and do a load of washing. Early enough?

YOU CAN'T HAVE IT ALL

At least most of us can't. My husband always says I can make Lincoln squeal as a way to talk about how tight I can be with money and how far I can make it stretch. It is a compliment and a criticism depending on the situation.

But back to the real issue. Most of us cannot buy or have everything we want or maybe what the neighbors have, or your friends at work. Many of us try. This can often get us in over our heads financially but what I think is even worse is that often by trying to live to everyone else's standards we cannot afford to buy the things we really want. The things that make us individuals. The things that really do define ourselves. For what really is money except for a tool to express who we are and what our priorities are? These can and will change during the course of our lives depending on our circumstances, available money, and time.

I now live far from the city suburban lifestyle. The farther out you go the more acceptable it is not to conform to the standards of others. None of the millionaires I have known have cared one wit about the clothes they wore as long as they were comfortable. Yet they could go out and buy anything they wanted with cash. This included new cars, diamonds, and land. Things that the majority of us are paying high interest rates to get.

So the key I have learned is to set your priorities. But more importantly is to admit and acknowledge the priorities you already have.

- You want a BMW? – get one.
- If hiking is your passion then get a pair of boots and head out.
- Never been to Hawaii? Then start planning.

A word about cheap. This word is often thrown as an insult at people who have much but don't throw around their money. Most often I have heard it used by someone that wanted something from the person that they didn't get so now they call them cheap. Be prepared. If you begin to save your money or buy things that others don't think they can afford the insults will start heading your direction. Mostly from, yes, you guessed it, relatives and friends. Jealousy and envy are strange things. Rather than asking how they too could do what you're doing some people instead will poke and prod with their insults. Because they are usually people close to us they know right where to hit us so that it will hurt. If you don't believe me just wait and see the reaction when you go buy the new boat or diamond bracelet you have been saving for. No need to mention that you gave up 3 years of eating out to get them.

The other route people take is to line up to borrow from you. A friend of mine had even the granddaughter's divorced father's new wife's daughter expecting to borrow money and then she got called cheap when she said no.

While we're on the subject, one of my favorite stories is Henny Penny. If you and your children haven't read it yet you might want to pick it up on your next trip to the library. Henny Penny sure was a tough old hen.

No, we can't have it all. But by prioritizing, planning, and cutting out the things that are really not that important to us we can have much more of that which we find truly satisfying.

WHAT ARE CLOTH DIAPERS?

Donna and Dave were a young couple with very little money. They were just trying to make ends meet. Dave had a minimum wage job and was trying to provide for his family the best he could. When Donna found out she was pregnant they were thrilled but not sure how they were going to make it. The family gave all kinds of advice on how to economize, how to budget, and suggestions about curbing expenses.

Donna's grandmother, Hazel, had raised five children herself on a scarce and unsteady income so she was very well aware of the challenges that lay ahead for the young couple. And, this would be their first great grandchild so it was a very exciting family event.

Hazel looked through all her fabric and began making all the basic baby items that would be needed. She sewed for hours and hours but it was a labor of love so every completed nightie or blanket was added to the ever growing pile. This baby was not going to go without. One of the biggest projects was to buy the fabric and make dozens of diapers. These were fashioned in the standard way with the modern inventions of Velcro to make them easy to adjust and take on and off. Since she was making them herself she not only used white fabric but also made some printed ones that matched the other outfits she had made. Even by making the diapers herself it was a big investment for their limited retirement income.

Finally, the big day arrived and no young mother could have been happier, but, neither could she be more inexperienced. Grandma went over every day for a while to help with the baby, housework, and the cooking. Donna had gotten some disposable diapers from the hospital in newborn size that she used when the baby first came home.

As the weeks passed Donna and Dave continued to have a hard time financially. Donna hardly had any energy since the baby arrived so Dave would often stop at McDonald's on the way home from work and pick up dinner to make it easier for Donna. He was a devoted husband and even helped with the housework. They continued to buy disposable diapers because by now they were used to them. Managing all the bills was getting harder and harder and Dave often worried. He wondered if he would even have money for gas. Once in a while a family member would help them out a little so they were able to get by.

After a few months passed they knew they had to do something different. They packed up the car for a short trip and went to Idaho, where they had more relatives, to look for jobs. They were so broke that they couldn't afford to buy Pampers so they packed up the cloth diapers that Donna's grandmother had made months ago.

They planned to make it a three-day trip and they stopped at McDonald's along the way for food. It was a wonderful treat even though they had to carefully watch their money. On the return trip home they were about 100 miles from home and it became obvious that they had misjudged the gas it would take. The gauge was on E and the money was gone.

Donna and Dave called their grandparents for help. Here they were, stuck and out of money. So grandma Hazel and grandpa went to the bank, got some cash and set out to rescue them. The grandparents couldn't believe that Donna and Dave had gotten themselves in this situation with the baby but nonetheless it was obvious that at this point they would have to save the scolding for later and just get them home safely.

When they met up, 100 miles from home, Hazel noticed that at least they were using the cloth diapers that she had spent so much time making. Common sense was hard to come by with these kids. It seemed like there was one step forward and two steps back. The baby needed to be changed so Hazel took on the task partly to assure herself that the baby was safe and sound. She asked Donna how the diapers worked out, how they fit, and began to tell Donna what she would have to do to wash them when she got home.

"Wash them?" Donna exclaimed. "I have been using them and throwing them away whenever we stopped".

This is a true story of one of my closest friends. At the time it happened and when she told me about it we just shook our heads hardly able to believe how dingy this granddaughter could be.

But the story is really no different from what many, in fact most, young couples are guilty of. Bills and other expenses are scrimped on in order to buy the disposable diapers. The major reason – washing cloth diapers is icky and gross. I can't deny that. But some things in life just are. The unpleasantness can be greatly reduced by buying the light weight diaper liners. It's no worse than changing the baby. Some things go with the territory and really aren't so bad when you get used to it. And, if washed properly the diapers are as clean as new.

Disposable diapers are great for trips, daycare, or if no laundry facilities are available. But they are an option. When finances are tight cloth diapers should definitely be considered. At least a couple dozen should be kept on hand for when expenses get tight. Pay your electricity, rent, and food first.

The money that can be saved using cloth diapers can even be used to start a college fund. Consider your options. An initial investment of about $100 is needed for cloth diapers. After that the cost will be under $5 per week for washing. Disposables cost about $20 per week. Over a two-year period as savings of about $1,400 can be achieved. It's an option.

UNCLAIMED PROPERTY

Here's an idea that is free, easy, and may surprise you. Get to a computer with Internet access. If you don't have one the library does. Enter your state name and "unclaimed property" in the search engine. This will take you to the states unclaimed property website. Enter you last name and if you have a common name the first initial of your first name. It will give you a list of all funds the state is holding under that name. Be sure and try all last names you have used and all states you have lived in.

By doing this I found money for four of my relatives and myself. Don't forget the names of relatives you have that have died. The topper was $1,200 for my husband. He had a great time buying a new TV and paid off a couple bills that he hadn't previously had the money for.

Try it. You might be surprised

CONSUMERISM

Being a consumer; something we are trained and proud to be. The government regularly reports it with the Consumer Price Index.

After hearing the word hundreds of times one day it really caught my attention. A consumer. What really is a consumer? As I pondered the word other words came to mind. To consume. Devour. Use up. We use the word when referring to fire. The fire consumed the building. Then I thought of other words. User, glutton, greedy, hoarder, waster. The dictionary also includes to destroy totally, to absorb. The more I thought on the word the more the meaning and practice sounded almost sinister. If I were to use these words about anyone else they would be offended, insulted, and think I was being critical. If I thought anyone had any of these characteristics I would consider it a shortcoming, a fault, and a vice.

Yet we take pride in our title. The government, media, and economists encourage us to be more of a consumer. But how can the continued act of destroying, using up, and devouring ever bring any ultimate progress or benefit either personally or nationally?

So I had to think it through again and am still thinking it through. The one thing I do know is that I don't want to be any of the things I listed above. I want to be a maker, restorer, builder, and display other similar characteristics in all that I do.

I have spent much time looking at my own life and habits to try to accomplish this. And though many so called conversationalists and environmentalists profess to want to achieve these objectives they seem more interested in telling other people to do it than doing it themselves if it is inconvenient. For example, it is easy to say that the rain forests should be saved compared to washing out your tin cans for recycle every time you use one. It is easy to talk about polluting our streams and rivers but do you break down and use pampers anyway. (Who wants to wash poopy diapers?) And of course we want the nation to conserve oil but not at the cost of us taking the bus.

On the news this morning I heard a report on the current drought conditions. The mayor of a large city asked everyone to flush one less time a day and turn off the water while brushing our teeth. What simple little things to do. Can it get much easier? But will everyone who heard the report do it? Very unlikely.

The lesson on consumerism was brought home to me years ago by the following situation: I had some extra bedding that was in good condition. The linen closet was too full so I put it in a box and into storage. A year went by and when I was cleaning I decided to see what I had in the box and if I could use any of it. When I opened the box it became obvious that the mice had gotten into it. There were smelly droppings and holes in what were once almost brand new items. I was disgusted. But most of all ashamed. Ashamed because I realized that someone who did not have any sheets could have used these and now through my hoarding they were good for nobody. Completely wasted and needing to be burned.

A consumer. A devourer. Is that really what we want to be?

It's tempting to look at the excesses of others and explain away why they are having financial difficulty.

Or if they are not having difficulty than we can comfort ourselves by telling ourselves that they are greedy and all they think about is money.

But really, this is not about anyone else. It is about looking at our own lives, expenses, and possessions and trying to look at them objectively enough to make some improvements in our decisions. I am not an advocate of never enjoying the money you make. I have a small Barbie doll collection. Just saying that means that to some people I am politically incorrect, to others extravagant, and to others eccentric. Oh well, the purpose of learning to manage our money more efficiently just may be to save enough on our coffee to buy another Barbie.

CHRISTMAS IN THE NORTHWEST

It's Christmas time and our TV has been on constantly. My husband is the kind who doesn't want to miss a thing.

Commercial after commercial tries to entice us to buy diamonds, printed boxers, and lots of electronic gadgets. This morning there was a news special highlighting how the malls are designed to encourage us to buy more. It showed how they use strategies designed to entice our five senses and even to get us lost and wandering, all in the attempt to motivate us to buy more. The last line of the sequence said something to the effect that if Americans only bought what we needed our whole economy would collapse.

In other reports the newscasters showed the food banks which had more and more people stopping in and not enough food on the shelves. Another report showed a woman in a nicely furnished apartment in Chicago who couldn't afford heat this year.

All the scenes melt together and the picture becomes confusing. And it happens every year.

The report that topped my attention was the one that said that the number one gift asked for by 8 years olds was a cellular phone. What? Do we ever stop and think about how ridiculous this all sounds? Probably not, because we are too busy worrying about whether we will be able to buy what we had hoped for each of our friends and family who we love. And, they definitely deserve any and all that we can give them because they are special to us.

Heat versus toys. Diamonds versus helping a stranger with Christmas dinner. Seems like it should be a simple decision but really it is not. We want it all. We deserve it all. And we surely don't want to be responsible for the collapse of the American economy, especially at Christmas time.

There is not a harder time of the year to reduce our expenses than Christmas time. We are literally bombarded with influences and enticements to spend. The expenses rise with property taxes and heat. Seasonal industries often experience layoffs. When money is the tightest we are most encouraged to spend, spend, and spend more. Is it any wonder that it is also the time of year that depression and suicide rises.

Whether we choose to spend or to cut back we end up feeling badly. The decisions we make now will affect how we go into the new year and it could take months to recover only to begin again the following year. As a teenager I remember a family who had the greatest Christmas. All the children got new bedroom sets and lots of clothes, TV's and other nice things. We had a modest Christmas and I felt that we must have been the poorest kids in the area. It wasn't until months later that I learned that the father of the family with the huge Christmas was laid off during the time he spent all this money. He had bought it all with credit and the whole family was now struggling because he still didn't have a job and the bills were continuing to mount up. I just didn't understand it and still don't. For even though this might be an extreme example it happens to most of us every year to some degree.

So what is the solution? We can live within our means and feel bad or we can spend more than we should and feel bad.

Almost every year we have gone through the Christmas challenge and feel like we have been beat up, stressed out and need to make apologies. The income gets reduced, unexpected bills come in, and we carefully try to select something each person will like. One time a friend saw me in the store while I was going through this process. I walked right by him without seeing him. He later told my husband that I looked like a zombie on a mission. Ever felt this way?

And then the presents. Every year I get carefully selected items that I don't need, don't fit, or I don't like. And I'm sure that people feel the same way about the presents I give. Each person gets a pile of stuff that they really could have done without. Every once in a while I have gotten a great gift and know that I have given them. But they are the exception, not the rule.

So where is this all leading? There really are no great solutions as far as I can see. The best advice I can give is to try every day of the season to give lots of smiles and lots of hugs to those you love. Some are going through hard times, some are stressed out, and some are sick. Smiles and hugs will strengthen, encourage, and remind us that life and love is worth living and love is worth giving. We can give them to friends, family, and strangers. If we give them with unlimited supply the season will be joyful.

IN SUMMARY

I could go on and on but my goal was to write a quick read. The stories I have shared are just the tip of the iceberg. There are some experiences that we have had during these years that I am just not ready to share. They would leave both you and I sobbing. So, if your situation seems more impossible or hopeless than ours was… maybe it is and maybe it isn't.

This book is not about despair, it is about hope. It is about the sunshine and rainbows that come after the storms of life.

I hope that the information provided will assist in your pursuit of meeting your family's needs, wants, and desires.

If the material has helped in any way or you would like to share your story or ask a question I would love to hear from you. The work on this book has been done by friends so you may find some areas of correction or improvement. I would be happy to consider them for a future printing if you would like to e-mail me.

Thanks for the time to share. If you would like more information or would like to share your stories email me at inthetrenches@live.com or check out the latest tips at our blog http://inthetrenches2009.blogspot.com .

SECTION C

**ALL FORMS MAY BE
REPRODUCED FOR
PERSONAL USE ONLY**

20___ Minimum Basic Budget

Minimum Basic	Jan	Feb	Mar	Apr	May	Jun	Jul	Aug	Sep	Oct	Nov	Dec	Total
Mortgage													0
Property Taxes													0
House Insurance													0
Car Payment													0
Car Insurance													0
Life Insurance													0
Electric													0
Phone													0
Credit Card Min Payment													0
Credit Card Min Payment													0
Sub Total	0	0	0	0	0	0	0	0	0	0	0	0	0
Optional Monthly													
Satellite													0
Internet													0
Debt Reduction													0
Sub Total	0	0	0	0	0	0	0	0	0	0	0	0	0
Expenses													
Apartment Rent													0
Food													0
Childcare													0
Pet Food													0
Sub Total	0	0	0	0	0	0	0	0	0	0	0	0	0
Priorities													
Total Expenses	0	0	0	0	0	0	0	0	0	0	0	0	0
Income													
Work													0
Other Income													0
Other Income													0
Total	0	0	0	0	0	0	0	0	0	0	0	0	0
Monthly Available	0	0	0	0	0	0	0	0	0	0	0	0	0

Does not include savings, reserve, spending.

20__ Expense Reduction Opportunities

	Monthly Reduction	Annual Reduction	Income
Total			

Priorities 20___

January		Cost	X
February		Cost	X
March		Cost	X
April		Cost	X
May		Cost	X
June		Cost	X
July		Cost	X
August		Cost	X
September		Cost	X
October		Cost	X
November		Cost	X
December		Cost	X

Goals 20__

		Estimated Cost
1		
2		
3		
4		
5		
6		
7		
8		
9		
10		
11		
12		
13		
14		
15		
16		
17		
18		
19		
20		

20__ Balance Sheet

Assets   ### Liabilities

Assets		Liabilities	
House		Mortgage	
Vehicle #1 Value		Vehicle #1 Amt owed	
Vehicle #2 Value		Vehicle #2 Amt owed	
Vehicle #3 Value		Vehicle #3 Amt owed	
Jewelry		Credit Card #1	
Furniture		Credit Card #2	
Savings		Credit Card #3	
Stocks		Personal Loan	

Total _____   _____

Net Worth   (assets minus liabilities) _____

JOB PROFITABILITY WORKSHEET

		Weekly	Monthly	1 year
Income/ Credits	Gross pay			
	Tips			
	Employee benefits			
	Employee discounts			
	One time Income/credits (put in 1 year column)			
	Total Income			
Expenses	Taxes			
	Gas			
	Clothes			
	Personal care products			
	Childcare			
	Lunches			
	Office expenses (gifts, parties)			
	Your special treats (coffee, morning donut) Other:			
	Total expenses associated with this job			
Net Income	Subtract expense total from income total			
Hours Spent	Work			
	Lunches			
	Commuting			
	Buying gas			
	Other:			
	Total hours			
Actual rate per hour	**Divide Net income by total hours**			

*the average monthly days worked is 21
Monthly hours worked is 173

NOTES

www.ingramcontent.com/pod-product-compliance
Lightning Source LLC
Chambersburg PA
CBHW051522170526
45165CB00002B/565